THE SPIDER'S WEB

BOOKS BY THE SAME AUTHOR

L'enfance gagnée (French)

Balance (English)

The King and the Widow –
One Thousand and One Camels (English)

Les trésors cachés (French)

EMILE TUBIANA

THE SPIDER'S WEB

Published by Le Pont International, Ltd.

Cover art and design:
Viviane Tubiana

LPI

Copyright © 2017 Emile Tubiana

All rights reserved. No part of this book may be reproduced, scanned, or distributed in any printed or electronic form without permission.

First edition: 1986
Second revised edition: December 2017
ISBN: 0991448820
ISBN-13: 978-0-9914488-2-1

TABLE OF CONTENTS

Preface	9
The Ballroom	11
John's Childhood	15
The Voyage	33
Josephine	70
India	91
The Estate	98
Sonia	130
The Hospital	158
Christina	186
The Tea Business	212
Back to Duty	236
Sonia's Plan	242
Conclusion	252

PREFACE

My purpose in writing this book was to illustrate how human experience differs with every individual according to the situation and the stages in his or her life. The feelings we all experience may be very similar, though triggered by quite different life experiences.

Every experience we encounter represents a trial, which has various effects on our lives and which we have to learn to overcome by recognizing our own feelings. Those feelings may pass unnoticed, as we do not know their value and their meaning. They are unveiled at various stages of our lives to prepare us for our next trial.

We often take our lives for granted. We do not realize that every day that we are alive and feel good is a day of grace. So many people in the world suffer from sickness; many are handicapped; many are hungry. They may seem far away from us, but they are part of us, and they deserve our attention and care. They share with us the same planet, the same air. Their existence is interconnected with ours, and our existence depends on their well-being.

I wrote my first book in my native language, French. *The Spider's Web* is my second book in English, for me, an acquired language. I must admit that I often had difficulty expressing my French thoughts in English, and it was sometimes very frustrating not to find the right word, despite an abundance of dictionaries. I often had to choose a word by compromise, not by conviction. My hope is that the message I wished to convey gets through.

THE BALLROOM

The ballroom was empty. John de Montaigne sat alone on his chair, his mind plunged in the distant past. The tables, covered with white cloth, were full of empty plates, glasses and bottles. The chairs had been left in disarray. A few napkins lay here and there on the floor. A coat, draped on a chair behind Mr. de Montaigne, had most likely been forgotten by a guest.

The head waiter stood next to the main entrance, awaiting Mr. de Montaigne's departure. It was already very late at night, but the head waiter did not dare disturb the famous host of the evening. Just a few hours ago, the ballroom had been filled with lively, animated and prominent guests, and John de Montaigne had just celebrated his sixtieth birthday. The most highly respected personalities of the city had been present. The city's Mayor, John Hudson, joined by his elegant and charming wife, had been present for the entire celebration. Mrs. Hudson was the second most famous personality after Mrs. de Montaigne.

The orchestra had been specially brought

in from New York. Such a magnificent and splendid party had never been seen since the days of European royalty. The ladies had been elegant in their beautiful evening dresses. The night had been a very special occasion for the younger ladies, who had come from distant places just to be seen. The guests had awaited and prepared for a long time, in expectation of this desirable exposure. The Mayor had not left the de Montaigne family for even a moment. He was proud to have had such a magnificent festivity in his city; the presence of a host of such stature had been an honor for his community. Every guest had tried to make his way towards the de Montaignes just to be noticed by one of the host's family members or his entourage. The guests had gossiped about the de Montaignes; some appeared to be envious.

The main ballroom of the hotel had never witnessed such a brilliant evening, replete with the richest and most influential families from all over the world. The brooding de Montaigne relived the entire evening in the now desolate ballroom. He seemed to be in deep thought. Just a few hours earlier, however, he had appeared to be the most radiant and happy man on earth. No one could have imagined that this would be

THE SPIDER'S WEB

his final evening with his family and friends. His entire wealth no longer held any importance for the silent host.

At present, everything hung by a thread. Mr. de Montaigne's future would be determined by a decision he was soon to reach. During the birthday ceremony, which he celebrated with the Mayor and his family, Mr. de Montaigne received a message, written on a small piece of paper, which he read avidly. Mr. de Montaigne continued hosting his party gracefully, as though nothing had happened to him. However, the message contained a few words upon which his entire life was now dependent.

Mr. de Montaigne had put the piece of paper in his pocket. No one had noticed any change in his facial expression. He had continued to be the charming and gracious host.

Now that he was alone, he reread those few words again and again. "My God, how could it be possible that everything had been based on falsehood?"

He must correct this. He did not know what to do with his family or with his wealth; it would be a painful decision. Yet he knew that he could not hesitate in making a prompt decision. His wife and his children had left with friends to continue the party at his magnificent residence. He knew that he could not divulge anything to anyone. His decision could shake the entire community. Thoughts about his children, his wife, and his business weighed heavily on his conscience. No one would understand his reason.

He chose to act silently, for he could not trust anyone. There was no one upon whom he could rely. All these thoughts crossed his mind, and suddenly he recalled all those terrible scenes that he had witnessed when he was only eight years old.

JOHN'S CHILDHOOD

At that time, John de Montaigne was living on a small farm in Louisiana with his mother and father. One day, while his mother was preparing the fire in the hearth, a spark accidentally ignited the rug. The fire quickly spread to the entire house, burning it to the ground. John's father had been unable to save his mother's life. She had perished in the flames, which lit up the entire neighborhood. His father chose to save John's life first. When he tried to go back into the blazing house to save his wife, it was John who had held him back.

"Daddy! Daddy! Daddy! Don't go! Think of me!" His father was desperate. He would have preferred to die with John's mother. In fact, it was John who had saved his father's life as the flames were raging, and it was already too late.

Afterwards, he traveled with his father from town to town, from state to state, searching for a new existence. His father did not even want to see farms anymore. John and his father became close companions. Their life became harder every day. His father sacrificed his entire life to raise John. He took care of him as well as his mother would have done. John never lacked anything except the love of his mother. He had everything he wanted from his father. However, no one could replace his beloved mother.

John and his father eventually left the American continent and landed in France. There, they moved from place to place, from city to city, looking for a new home and livelihood. They spent their first two years moving, with all their worldly possessions, from hotel to hotel.

The elder de Montaigne did almost anything to earn a living. John, who had never before left the farm, began to acquaint himself with this new way of life. The evenings were the saddest moments for him. It was very hard for the young boy to forget his mother. He listened attentively to every conversation that his father had with other businessmen. He was mature for his age, but never showed it or interfered in any discussion. Finally, they settled in Paris, and from there they traveled every week to various cities. After he had tried many different businesses, the senior de Montaigne became a spice merchant.

One day, while visiting a customer, they met an English gentleman, Mr. Mershenson, who worked for a British company that dealt mostly in tea. He was also a widower, and the two men became close friends.

John was thirteen years old when they settled in Paris, and he had to start school again. It was not easy for the young boy to begin a steady way of life, especially after all he had been through.

John was often sad, and sometimes he had a feeling of nostalgia. He did not know why his soul was invaded by such feelings. He felt as though he was a stranger everywhere. His father never displayed any feelings of sadness, but John knew that his father suffered from the loss of his wife. John was burdened by having to adapt himself to both a new language and a new way of life, but he had to spend his time in serious study. He never played with his classmates. He was isolated within himself. His teacher took a liking to him and always tried to help him.

During his first school year, John studied remarkably well. He spoke French almost like a Frenchman, with a slight American accent. Eventually, John and his father became French citizens. Mr. Mershenson was the only friend that the de Montaignes had, and he was always welcome in their home. Mr. de Montaigne's business had prospered year after year, but his earnings were just enough to cover school costs and their daily needs. Mr. de Montaigne had always dreamed about and awaited something big to happen. His main concern was to ensure a happy life for his son, John. Mr. Mershenson, who came to Paris once a month, suddenly ceased to appear. The de Montaignes kept hoping that he would show up again one day. They traveled many times to England, hoping to find their good friend Mershenson. The elder de Montaigne had corresponded with him on a regular basis. One day, his letter to Mr. Mershenson came back marked "address unknown". The letter caused both de Montaignes much concern and pain. After a while, they gave up hope that they would ever see their friend again. After that, Mr. de Montaigne did not make any new friends.

John became a fine gentleman; he was highly educated and cultivated in every respect of life. The young ladies found him attractive, but he never wanted to be attached to any young girl of his age. He often dreamed of enchanting a woman like his mother, but deep in his heart he preferred not to think about this delicate subject. The trauma of his mother's death was still fresh in his mind.

He remembered the day when his father had

announced the exciting news to him about a long trip that they would be taking together.

When John was nineteen years old, his father had received a strange letter from India. The senior de Montaigne could not figure out who could have sent the letter. When he opened it, he felt his heart leap, for he recognized the handwriting of his friend Mershenson. During his long period of absence from Europe, Mr. Mershenson had settled in India and had invested his money in a tea plantation. He had become a rich man. The letter contained a warm invitation to the de Montaignes to come to India.

"Do you know your geography?" asked the father. "Do you know where India is?" John could pinpoint every country on the map. He knew even more than his father had imagined. The senior de Montaigne was going to realize his old dream, especially having now become a good tea and spice merchant in the newly emerging and rapidly growing trade with India.

The senior de Montaigne, who had dreamed of a business coup for a long time, saw an opportunity to make his biggest deal with his friend, in this invitation. John did not know about the letter when his father had asked him the question about India. He could not imagine even for a moment the reasons behind his father's plans for a long trip. But John also dreamed about something new, an adventure which would lead him to something yet unknown. Meanwhile, his father had already made all the necessary preparations for the long journey. He bought new light clothes for John and himself, and a large trunk.

"John, pack enough clothes and books to read for at least six months," said his father, "we are going to India! Our friend Mershenson has a tea plantation! Can you imagine?" His father repeated these words again and again. John was pleasantly surprised with the good news. His mind delved into the history lessons that he had learned. He knew little about India. He knew only about the high Himalayan Mountains and about India's ancient culture. India was a land of many languages and religions and a nation with a large population, with many Princes and Princesses. India was the homeland of many Gods, where poverty and wealth were neighbors. But John was aware that all this knowledge was very limited for such a trip.

John tried to hide his excitement about the voyage. He was moved. His body quivered, and he sensed mixed feelings of joy and dismay.

He looked at his father's face with happiness, devotion, and piety. All these tender feelings revived once again the sensations that he had experienced the day after his mother had died. Although he had only been a boy at the time, he had felt the sorrow and depression that had surrounded his father. At that time the entire world seemed strange to him; he wanted to disappear somewhere far away, just to stop these strange feelings which had invaded him and made him so unhappy. He felt the earth tremble under his feet; he had been uprooted by everyone and everything. He tried to escape from himself without success. Sentiments of varying degrees of gloom had agitated his soul. He knew that no one could understand or allay his grief. Even the priest had not inspired confidence in him.

John had not been able to understand why such a tragedy had happened to him. He had felt innocent. When the priest invoked God, John almost fought against the thought of invoking God for every single thing. God has nothing to do with such an accident. All these thoughts crossed his mind in a matter of seconds. Now he realized that somewhere, sometime he would be rewarded for all those past moments of pain. He recognized that something beyond his control was alive. Such a positive thought gave him confidence. The senior de Montaigne could not have imagined at the time what was going on in his son's mind and soul.

John did not disclose any of his thoughts to his father. He was very pleased for him. Maybe something would finally make his father happy. But at the same time John felt sorrow for his father, as he would now finally see the fulfillment of his long overdue dream, but not with his dear wife at his side. John could not tell if his feelings of sorrow came from his father's loneliness or were within himself. He wanted to express his satisfaction, but he felt anxiety and a sense of fear that someone may have been observing him. He chose not to divulge his happiness for fear of losing the joy which came to him and to his father as a result of their dear friend Mershenson's invitation. John could not trust anyone in the world except his father and Mr. Mershenson, both of whom knew of suffering and pain, as both had lost their dear wives.

John felt a sadness similar to the one he had experienced upon the death of his mother. However, this time it seemed to be blended with a nuance of happiness, leading John to realize that sadness and happiness are related and that they originate from the same source.

Now he enjoyed every minute of his life. He suddenly realized that in all those years he had never noticed the taste or smell of the air he breathed. The air that penetrated his lungs seemed to infuse John with a new sensation. He suddenly started to realize that he, too, was alive, that some justice did, after all, exist.

He began to understand that God had nothing to do with his mother's death; that through John's warning, God had saved his father from the fire. He reasoned that all of those warnings mentioned in the Bible were not issued with any spirit of punishment, but with a spirit of concern and caring. The sign "Danger", which confronts us in many places, is for our own protection and is parallel to the Biblical guides.

How could any child be safe if his parents did not instruct him about danger and prudence? The human race has created so many things for our advancement and prosperity, but those creations can also be dangerous even for those who presently know how to apply and master them. Societal rules are there to maintain order, just as the universe operates with certain laws.

John began to understand that no creation could be achieved without various diverging forces. The real question is how to master these forces. When one discovers the correct way, the right ingredients, the exact dosage, the true density and the best rhythm, then one can create beautiful things on earth. These consist of exquisite music, a perfect design, a colorful painting, the most sensitive poems and so many other things which make us happy, pleased, and satisfied and awaken us from our deep dreams.

John was now radiant; his handsome face glowed with color. The senior de Montaigne was busy preparing all kinds of documents for the forthcoming trip. John did not inform anyone about their future plans.

Suddenly Paris, that beautiful city where he had spent most of his childhood, did not have any meaning for him anymore. John spent his last days there studying the world map, tracing the journey with his pencil, jotting a few notes here and there, searching for information about each and every place to which he might have to travel. He eagerly read about the Suez Canal, which was now becoming used as a faster way to get to the Indian Ocean.

His reading about the Suez Canal triggered his interest in Egypt, about which he now avidly gathered information. He remembered a story from the Holy Bible, which his father had told him. A canal linking the Mediterranean to the Red Sea had long been a cherished idea, and many credited the Pharaoh Necho who had attempted in his day to build a Suez Canal, but it was Napoleon who had revived the idea of a shorter trade route to India via the Suez Canal. The human undertaking fascinated John. His father had also told him about the Pharaohs, the Pyramids and the Israelites. At that time, his father had wished to strengthen John's faith. After his daily work, the Bible had been de Montaigne's only hobby.

One day, before his exams, John was very nervous, although he had revised very carefully for his exams. He did not feel confident. He particularly remembered the story about Moses and the children of Israel.

"You see, John, we are always afraid of the next day and of the future," his father had said. "Let me tell you a story about the Israelites in the desert. After the people of God had faced so many obstacles, and despite God's many miracles, they were still complaining to Moses. One day they were subjected to a new trial; there was no food to eat, so they again lamented to Moses, who spoke to God and asked for advice.

God performed another miracle. This time he created 'Manna' (the bread from Heaven). The people from the Desert were unappeased and groaned, 'What kind of God is this, who gives us only one kind of food to eat?' Moses, upon hearing their protest, again called upon God.

"God replied, 'Moses! Moses! Do you think I do not hear? Tell my people that this Manna contains every conceivable taste; while they eat they will savor any meal they desire' Once again Moses was happy to convey God's message.

"The Israelites who were concerned about the next day, had stored as much Manna as they could. The next morning, the holy bread had rotted and was infested with worms. Again the children of God were furious. 'What kind of God is this, who gave us bread that rots?'

"Moses, sensing their fury, again addressed God. Then he suddenly heard God's voice, louder than it had ever been. 'Moses! Moses! Do not my people trust me even for one day? If I was able to create Manna yesterday, can I not create it again today?' Moses was both ashamed and embarrassed at having conveyed such a message to God."

John's father continued, "My son, if you have been successful in so many exams in the past, what makes you doubt your success this time?" John understood what his father was attempting to illustrate. His message was, "Have confidence in tomorrow." The next day John passed his exams with high honors. From that moment on, he regained his self-confidence. Thus, John enjoyed such tales from the Bible every night, embellished by his father's comments.

Because the Bible had made such an impression upon John, the history of Egypt and the Suez Canal held an even greater fascination. John was most impatient to see the great manmade waterway, which connected the Mediterranean to the Red Sea, while hoping to discover the Pyramids and other places referred to in the Bible.

John's mind teemed with dreams and curiosity. There was so much to read. He had never been so eager to study history as he was now.

Mr. de Montaigne, who usually inspired John with his serenity and wisdom, now appeared quite different. John could discern a sign of happiness and nervousness in his face, but he could not pinpoint the kind of thoughts passing through his father's mind. Once in a while, his father would interrupt the silence with a sentence like, "I think we will have a good time there." His words seemed to hide his feelings. John sensed that his father now wanted to strengthen and justify his spontaneous decision of making their forthcoming trip. He looked in his father's eyes, but this time his father's visual expression had changed slightly. He even tried to avoid John's observant gaze, and as he turned his face, he said, "You know, John, you will discover so many new things. Perhaps you will even meet a nice girl!"

John was reticent about responding to his father's words. He knew that his father just wanted to break the silence. Mr. de Montaigne could not realize what this trip would mean to John. He thought his decision to make the trip might have a negative impact on the young boy. Because John knew and understood his father very well, he began to feel sorry for him. He wanted to prevent his father from vacillating further. In order to reinforce his father's decision, John decided to break the ice, "Father, do you know how proud I am to have a father like you? I have been anticipating such a momentous decision for so many years." His father's expression started to change; he looked happy this time. John had cleared the air. Both de

THE SPIDER'S WEB

Montaignes now felt relieved and comfortable. John continued, "Father, I am happy to leave Europe and to discover a new world. You will also be happy there."

Although he knew very little about India, John felt a kind of warmth spreading through his heart at the mere thought of going to India. He was more excited than his father could imagine. He experienced the feelings of someone returning home after a long period of exile. He could not understand the existence of such unknown emotions. Had his father's stories awakened those feelings that John had never been prepared for? John looked at his father with a sweet smile and said, "Father, can you tell me a story about Jesus?"

Mr. de Montaigne, pleased to hear John's request, replied, "Do you remember the story about Jesus when he was young?"

John, filled with curiosity, replied "Do you mean when he went to India to study?"

John's father knew that he had never told such a story; in astonishment he asked John, "Who told you such a story? Jesus never went to India! He went to Egypt with his parents when he was still a baby. At that time his father was looking for work in Egypt."

John, wanting to confirm what he had once heard, answered, "Oh yes, Father, he did study in Egypt, right?"

Mr. de Montaigne was shocked by John's version and he corrected his son. "In the first place, Jesus never went anywhere to study. If someone wants to study, he need not go anywhere. Knowledge is in our hearts; we just have to dig deep enough. If we just discover our heart's language we will not need to study anymore. You are confusing my stories with someone else's. I know that there is a story about seven men who came from India to visit Jesus, in Judea, of whom three were very close to him. They initiated him so that he found himself. Everyone tells a story in his own way, there is nothing wrong with it. Everyone also understands the truth as he chooses. In reality there is only one truth, and he who finds it will have to keep it to himself."

John interrupted his father, "Father, do you think it is worth making such a big effort, only with the hope that your friend may help you in your business?" Mr. de Montaigne, who did not get to tell his story about Jesus, found in John's question the best opportunity to begin his tale.

"One day, Jesus was walking through the desert with his disciples. The sun blazed so strongly that everyone began to lose his strength. They were all parched and exhausted. One of the disciples saw a coin lying on the sand but was too lazy to bend down for it. Jesus, who was walking behind him, bent down himself and picked up the coin. In a little while they reached a small village. None of them had any money to buy anything. Jesus, who had the coin, bought cherries. He continued walking, while throwing cherries behind him, one at a time. The same disciple, who had not bent down for the coin, now bent down to pick up every cherry."

John understood the message and said to his father, "I will bend down even for a small coin. I may find a use for it."

"If we are invited, why should we refuse, or doubt our friend Mershenson?" answered the elder de Montaigne, with his usual calmness.

John did not wish to disturb his father's hope and dream, although he was not convinced by his father's argument. In order not to arouse a controversy with his father, and because he wanted to appease him, John said, "Father, you are right, we have only one true friend in this world." His father simply smiled without reaction. He seemed to understand John's allusion. "Our best friend is always there when we need him", said

John's father calmly.

This conversation between father and son was the first one of its kind. Both de Montaignes were now silent and looked one another in the eyes. Both men were content and felt the joy without having to say a word. John went to bed and sought to find a way to remember the joy his father had evoked in him, until his thoughts were taken over by sleep.

THE SPIDER'S WEB

THE VOYAGE

It was on a Wednesday that John and his father embarked on a newly built steamer. John was as excited as a little boy. On his first trip, when he had taken the ship from New York, John had been sad and afraid of everything. Now that he was an adult, John was acutely aware of every facet of the trip. His father had booked a nice stateroom, with two beds on the third deck of the ship. The vessel was modern in comparison to the first one. This time John was full of hopes for the future. His attitude was most positive; he found everything stimulating.

After settling in their cabin, John was eager to familiarize himself with the ship, while his father preferred to relax in their stateroom. He explored every deck; he even visited the boiler room. He was consumed by curiosity. He knew that they would have to spend many weeks in their temporary floating home. He remembered his first transatlantic crossing which had brought him from America and felt as though he had never left the ship since his boyhood. It was as though he was forged with the ship and the sea. All those years that he had spent in Europe were now erased from his memory. He sensed a strong attraction to the ship, although he had never seen this ship before. On his first trip, the direction of the ship had been from West to East. This time, their course was the same.

The main port of Marseilles was surrounded by many large buildings facing its water, calm as a lake, reflecting the blueness of the sky. Many trawlers, passenger and merchant ships, created a lively atmosphere. Freight, crates, and people of diverse nationalities headed in different directions, had contributed their colors to the decor of the bustling city.

All this tumult went unnoticed by John. His mind was plunged into the journey ahead and into the future. He was so completely absorbed that he forgot all about Paris, his school, and his friends. Everything around him seemed like a dream. All the sufferings and sad moments that he had endured were now nonexistent. He did not even want to enter into conversation with the other passengers. He was content to remain alone looking at the sky and the water. He did not realize that he had already been on the ship for three hours; the time had passed quickly and without his notice. The ship was still anchored at the pier. Many families and friends were waving farewell to their relatives and loved ones. These gestures made John realize that the ship had now truly begun to move. The colorful houses surrounding the port also started to move. John could not figure precisely which were really moving, the houses or the ship. Slowly, slowly, the port became a picturesque panorama. The people on the pier became smaller and smaller.

He felt the ties of the rope which bound him to the vessel. Although this liner was much more modern than the one which had brought him to Europe, he could not sense any difference. It is amazing how one can become so attached to a new location, that one can forget any other place in which one has lived for a long period of time.

John also felt like he was trapped by the magnetic forces, the ship, and the sea. This time he was going happily towards the unknown. Deep within himself, he knew that he had to go, although he himself had not made the decision to take the trip. He felt that he was being carried downstream like a small fish in a river. Any resistance would be to no avail. He knew he could not have changed the course of this trip even if he had wanted to do so. But he did not offer any resistance. Just to go – that had been his dream, although he could not anticipate what unknown destiny awaited him. He did not even realize that he had been separated from his beloved father. For a moment he sensed that he had no control over his future, but he was pleased with these feelings. He was immersed deeply in his thoughts and did not realize that the sun had started to set, making way for nightfall. The ship was already on the open sea. John could see the mountains on the horizon. A few stars began to light up the sky. Now the ship was enveloped in obscurity. There was no difference between the sea and the sky, only that the sky had its brilliant inhabitants.

Mr. de Montaigne, who had been searching for John, was now loudly calling, "John! John!" When he reached his son's side, John appeared to be awakening from a dream. "John! I have been looking for you for hours! Didn't you hear me?"

John who was a little embarrassed about having forgotten his father, replied, "I am sorry, Father, I was admiring the sea."

"It is time for dinner." The sweet smell of the sea started to permeate the dining room. John could distinguish a slight difference between the smell of the Atlantic and the Mediterranean. This time the odor of iodine was accentuated. Even his lungs seemed to breathe better.

After dinner, John would have preferred to stay outside in the fresh sea air, but he realized that he couldn't again leave his father alone. Now, as John lay on his bed, the ship began to develop a swaying movement which tickled his stomach.

The sea was churning and agitated. The waves, which had almost been calm before, now started to rock the ship. As the ship proceeded, the movement became unpleasant. Mr. de Montaigne, who until then had never been sick, began to vomit. John, who had never experienced such seasickness, became upset. The delicious dinner that they had had for the first time on the ship had become a dead weight in Mr. de Montaigne's stomach. Soon, their lovely stateroom was covered with retching. John had to clean his father like a baby. His father's condition worsened every minute. John spent his time cleaning the cabin, changing to fresh towels; the smell became insufferable. John had never seen his father sick before. This was the first time that he was faced with such a situation. As long as he had known his father, he had never had to take care of him. Now, he was alone; his father was suffering a great deal, and his face had turned green. John became nervous for the first time in his life. Until then, his father had taken care of him when he had been sick. John felt miserable, and all kinds of thoughts made him perceive the sense of life around him. He had always taken his father's good health for granted in the past. He had never thought that his father might get sick.

Although John loved his father, he had never experienced a feeling of sorrow for him. He had never thought that his father might die. As he observed his father's struggle with pain, he suddenly became aware that he might lose his beloved father. This thought made him even sadder.

He did not close his eyes for even a moment. His main concern and prayers were for his father's life. The thought that he might become an orphan revived thoughts of the day that his mother died. The tickling in his stomach that he had first felt after dinner suddenly disappeared in the face of the new reality. He could not see anything through the portholes, but he could hear the wind battering against the side of the ship. The vessel behaved like a small box on a lake. The long-awaited trip that he had dreamed of had suddenly become an unwanted event. He now wished that the trip had never taken place. The thought that his father might die precipitated feelings of abject fear in John. He realized how much his father now needed his help. He could not remember ever having seen his father ill, even during the first trip which had brought them from America.

John was tired, frightened, and sad. Just before the break of dawn, his father's pains seemed to ease. John lay down on his bed to get a little relaxation, so he would be ready to help his father. At that moment, he remembered the story that his father had told him one day when John asked him why he was so good to him. His father had answered thus:

"There was once a rich merchant who had worked through his entire life just to increase the fortune that his own father had left him. He was a miserly man. His priest's visits ceased to be frequent, as he always turned down requests for charity to the poor. A few days before his death, the merchant suddenly remembered the priest. He asked his children to call him. However, the priest could not be reached anywhere that day. The wealthy man realized that his fortune would not help save his life. He requested that his children call his lawyer. When the lawyer came to his bedside, the rich man told him to change his last will and testament to read that he would donate his entire fortune to the church and the poor after his death. A few days later, the rich old man did, indeed, die.

"At that moment, the Angel of Death came to lead him on his way to his new abode. The Angel and the wealthy man entered a dark tunnel. The Angel followed behind the merchant. The rich man kept tripping from time to time like a blind man. After a while of suffering and groping in the dark, the rich man turned to observe how the Angel was making his way, and to his surprise he discovered that the Angel had been holding a bright candle to light his path. The rich man had been accustomed to giving orders during his lifetime. He thus commanded the Angel:

"'Please come forward with your candle, so that I can see my way!'

"The Angel replied, 'I am sorry, I cannot break the law.'

"The rich man became furious when he realized that for the first time in his life his orders were not being obeyed at all. In a loud voice, he screamed at the Angel, 'What is this powerful law of yours that I have to break my neck in this darkness?'

"The Angel calmly replied, 'The light is only for those who are charitable.'

"The rich man, remembering his testament, then said to the Angel, 'Do you know who I am?'

"'Yes!' answered the Angel.

"The merchant was not satisfied with the Angel's answer and continued, 'You must be mistaken. I am the most generous person in the world. I have left my entire fortune to the church and the poor.'

"The Angel asked, 'When will the church and the poor receive this fortune?'

"The merchant was relieved, for he now believed that the Angel had not been aware of his testament. He would certainly apologize for his mistake. He replied, 'Right now, after my death.'

"The Angel answered sweetly, 'Now I understand why I received instructions to follow you with the lit candle.'

"The rich man became quite happy and in the voice of a greatly honored man, said to the Angel, 'All right, I excuse you. You see, charity is light. Now please come forward and light my way.'

"The Angel again proceeded to a question, 'Have you given your entire fortune as you said?'

"'Yes, sir,' answered the merchant proudly.

"'When? Was it during your lifetime?' continued the Angel

"'Oh, yes!' swore the rich man.

"'When will the church and the poor benefit from your fortune, sir?'

"The rich man became impatient and furious with this annoying Angel's questions and shouted loudly, 'What are all these questions for? I will complain to your superior.'

"The Angel answered firmly, 'I receive my instructions only from the Eternal Law itself. And that Law can never be wrong.'

"The rich man, who used to be respected, believed that the Angel was trying to wrangle with him and continued, 'It is best that you come forward. I will forgive you.'

"The Angel answered, 'I now understand that you have willed your entire fortune to be used after your death; that is why I am holding the candle behind you. You are now dead. Had you deeded your fortune for use while you were still alive, the light of the candle would have been before you and would have lighted your way.'

"The rich man felt that he had been cheated and, with the disappointment sensed by an astute businessman, he said to the Angel, 'I will call my lawyer and tell him to change the testament.' He now realized that all this harangue had not impressed the Angel or changed his mind. He suddenly thought of another solution and told the Angel in a patronizing voice, 'I understand. You are a poor man who always leads the way for the dead. I should have realized that before. Come forward with the light and I will take care of you.' The Angel did not even bother to answer.

"The dead man now realized that the Angel was very loyal to his superior and could not be bribed with money. He understood that the only language that the Angel would accept was charity. He regretted having spent his entire life ignoring the priest's exhortations for funds when he had so much money."

John now thought about the meaning of his father's story. This tale had awakened in him the will to do good while there was still time.

Mr. de Montaigne seemed to be relieved of pain and was in deep sleep. Now, for the first time, John experienced a sense of responsibility. He realized how much his father had suffered in silence for all those years since the death of his wife. He remembered how many times he had himself been sick and how much his father had taken care of him with love and devotion.

John now felt that he was no longer a child. He had become an adult. He promised himself that from now on he would take on his father's responsibilities. He would give him all the love in the world. He was angry with himself for not having realized sooner that his father also needed love and care. He felt a sense of guilt. His father had sacrificed his life for him. He should have married another woman. He now wished that this trip would end as quickly as possible so that he could reward his father for all the love, goodness and care that he had lavished on John for so many years.

John realized why his father had told him the story of the Merchant and the Angel. The ship moved with a constant speed. Father and son had missed their first sunrise together on the high seas, as both were now immersed in deep sleep after such an agitated night.

When John awoke, the sea was calm and it was broad daylight. The night before, seemed like a bad dream. All the bad feelings and sense of regret that he had felt had dissipated with the storm. Now he felt like his old self again. He could not understand how his feelings of responsibility and sorrow had disappeared with the arrival of daylight. He understood for sure that one could not ignore one's own feelings. The experience was probably necessary and taught him that he would have to take fuller responsibility for his own life. His father was still soundly asleep and seemed in no pain, and John stood next to him and observed him for a while.

This was the first time that he had seen his father in profound slumber. The temptation to go out on deck was strong. He hesitated for a moment in his thoughts, then suddenly decided to get dressed fast. He took a glimpse through the porthole, where he could see the calm blue sea. The ship was moving smoothly now. He put on a sweater over his shirt and went out. When he saw the well-dressed passengers on deck, admiring the sea, John felt that he had missed something precious. He then realized that he had missed his first sunrise at sea.

He felt sorry that the night before he had been ready to give up all this new source of happiness, and was ready to return to Paris. Now the beauty of the turquoise sea combined with the blue of the sky added to his long overdue dream. All the passengers were completely unknown to him, but they all had something in common: they were all headed towards something new, although each had his own purpose. He realized that all these passengers were different from the people that he had known before. They had more experience and they were all more open to the world, with its various facets, people and languages.

He wished that this journey would last longer because these feelings in the middle of the sea were a very special experience and certainly better than the dark feelings of regret and melancholy that had prevailed before.

John breathed deeply of the pure air with a little of the special smell from the sea; it made his trip agreeable and full of dreams and hope. His enthusiasm had been revived to an even higher degree than he had yet known. The medley of passengers, the ship, the sea, the sky and the sun formed a beautiful panorama in variegated blue.

This first day aboard ship was shorter than usual, as John and his father had slept all morning. His father finally joined him on deck. John now cherished him like a child. Mr. de Montaigne had never before experienced John taking care of him.

They spent the day walking from deck to deck, admiring the blue sea. When evening came, John and his father were hungry, as they had abstained from food all day long. Meanwhile, John had spoken to many sailors, and one of them had given him much good advice on how to prevent seasickness. When John and his father went to dine in the lavishly decorated dining room, John recalled the advice of the sailor who had told him to avoid liquids. John, who had not forgotten the previous night, thus advised his father to order only sandwiches. After dinner they spent a couple of hours admiring the stars which had begun to appear while they were dining.

A sense of calmness and serenity prevailed on the deck of the vessel. John again experienced the warmth of his father's presence. Though he had been eager the night before to take over the responsibility of his father's life, he was not yet ready to give up the daily bedtime story that his father used to tell him. He observed his father for a while to reassure himself that his health and spirits were in good shape. He felt, more than ever before, the need to hear his father narrate stories, and he also felt the need to commit them to memory as soon as possible. Then John smiled at his father complacently and said, "Father, can you tell me a story today?" Mr. de Montaigne seemed glad to hear John's request, as in the old days.

"What would you like to listen to, today?"

John hesitated for a while, then took his

courage in his hands and said, "Father, you have never told me how you met Mother."

This question awakened his father's interest, although he was ready for sleep after his first exciting day at sea. He first looked John deeply in the eyes, as though he wanted to tell him, "Oh! My son, this is the most incredible story in my life." John sensed that something was passing through his father's mind. He thought at first that maybe his father was not yet ready to reopen the old wounds and awaken the painful memories. Then his father's voice interrupted his thoughts. "John, I am glad to hear your request; I have waited so long for this question." He sighed and continued, "I was deeply disturbed and sad when I met your mother. It was early in the afternoon, on a normal weekday; the sun shone brightly, everything seemed as usual; one could not imagine that this would be the turning point of my life. At that time I had been seeing another girl for more than a year; we loved each other very much. We were two inseparable human beings. She had sworn that our relationship would last forever.

"On that day, we had a rendezvous in what was then the marketplace. I was the first to arrive. This was not usual; normally she had always been first. I waited for over an hour. No sign of Josephine."

John interrupted, "Who is Josephine?"

"The girl that I am talking about," replied his father, somewhat annoyed by John's question, and continued, "As I said, she had not arrived; I became nervous, because I knew that she was always on time. Many bad thoughts passed through my mind. I tried to calm myself by thinking of various positive possibilities. But something kept nagging at me; I thought of an accident; or maybe she was sick; something must have happened to her.

"Another hour passed, and then my heart started to tremble with joy when her silhouette appeared at the other side of the marketplace. I prayed with relief. I had thanked God for the happiest day of my life, when suddenly I realized that Josephine was walking towards me very slowly. I thought of running towards her, but held myself back, as I did not want to appear ridiculous, since the place was full of people who knew us both.

"I decided to remain where I was, but Josephine's steps were even slower and the short distance which separated us became endless. When her face was just a short distance from mine, I perceived her eyes, which were not smiling as usual this time. I again experienced a sense of concern. I had thought that something must have happened in her family. But I never thought at that minute that something had happened which would change my entire life.

"The need to kiss her and hug her was so strong that my whole being shook violently. I tried to hide my emotions, but my face must have surely betrayed me. When she reached me, she stopped short. I tried to restrain myself, in order to give her the chance to talk first. Her face had changed drastically. Her expression was serious; she was silent and seemed very concerned about how to break the news to me. I decided to comfort her without knowing why.

"'Don't worry, Josephine, I am with you in good things and bad.' As I finished saying these words, her expression became even more clouded. This time she seemed to express pity for me. I thought that the news would be terrible and that Josephine was trying to protect me from a great shock.

"I thought at that moment about her mother and father; something must have happened which had made her silent with shock. I was at a loss about how to finally extract the bad news from her. Every moment of silence became an eternity.

"Then, with a feigned smile, she began, 'It is a nice day today.'

"I understood then that something had happened that had made her change. I realized, too, that the reason could not be so bad after all. Then I thought she might be playing a game with me. I said to her angrily, 'For God's sake, what happened to you?' She continued to smile; this time I could see that her smile contained a hint of irony. And then suddenly I remembered that she had once told me a joke, in order to determine if I was a jealous person. I had refused to be serious and had played along. But I could not begin to realize that this time it was in earnest. Suddenly, I felt like a stranger. The entire ground seemed to heave under my feet. This time if we were playing a game, then it was going to be a long one.

"She had always cared about my feelings before and had never pushed so far. Usually, she had been the one to run towards me like a child. Her presence used to enliven my whole being. Her vitality used to give me a lot of strength and courage. Today, this seemed to have changed and I could not figure out why. My mind was in total confusion. Josephine continued, 'The sun is my best friend.' I had not heard the word 'sun', just the word 'friend'. I hat not understood what she meant. My emotions, at that moment, filled not only my entire body, but also my brain, which was not functioning at all.

"I just remember that at that time I repeated the word 'friend'.

"She did not lose a moment and said, 'Yes, I have a new friend.'

"Meanwhile, I tried to analyze her sentence quickly in my mind. I then recalled that she had mentioned 'The sun is my best friend.' I repeated after her, 'Yes, the sun is our best friend.'

"She smiled again and repeated, 'You are not listening. I have a new friend.' I thought she wanted to tell me that she had discovered something new in me that she had not realized before and which she wanted to express particularly and specially by saying, 'I have a new friend.' Then, in order to try and to be on her intellectual level, I continued, 'Of course, you have now discovered both the old and the new friend.'

"'Yes,' she answered, very pleased that I had finally understood what she had been trying to say. She then continued, 'I want to introduce him to you.'

"'Of course,' I answered, believing that I had understood what was going on in her head, when she suddenly turned her head to the right and called,

"'Matthew, will you come here, I want to introduce you to my old friend.' I was numb with shock and did not want to draw any conclusion. It must be that she wanted to introduce me to a cousin whom I did not know, and this game was aimed at testing my feelings. Like a stupid, I greeted this young man enthusiastically. Then, suddenly, she kissed him on the lips.

"There was no longer any doubt. This was not a game, but hard reality. I was paralyzed by the new situation. Josephine turned towards me and gave me a lovely kiss. I was completely confused and could not understand what was happening to me. The situation became even more complicated when she again gave Matthew a kiss on the mouth. This time, the kiss continued as though I was not even present. When she saw that I did not react, Josephine said, 'You see, I knew that you would understand. I love you both with all my heart.'

"The word 'confused' no longer held any meaning for me. I could not begin to realize what was happening to me. Then I suddenly became aware that Josephine really meant what she was saying. I had one of two choices. Either to accept this new situation, which was to share Josephine with this young man, or to take the consequences and to quit. My feelings were in turmoil and my blood was boiling like lava. I suddenly wanted to quit, but somehow the words did not come out. I had lost my composure. I looked in her eyes and felt that I loved her much more than before, but I did not have the courage to tell her what I was thinking. The truth was that I myself did not know what to decide. I glanced at the new friend. I pitied him. I did not want to hurt him. I did not want to hurt her either. At that moment, I did not think about myself. The more I looked at her, the more beautiful she seemed. I wanted to kiss her and hug her. I discovered more details in her face than I had ever discovered before.

"If this man had not been there I would have been the happiest man in the world, but his presence disturbed my tranquility. She was watching me with expectation. I saw in her eyes that she also loved me more. The young man was watching to see my reaction. We must have had similar thoughts. He was good. He was nice. He was younger than I. 'My God,' I said to myself, 'what should I do?' Then suddenly the feeling of pardon came to my heart. If I loved her so much, I should not disturb her happiness. I thought the best thing was to let her be happy with her new man.

"Finally, love means to give and not to take. So I traded my happiness for hers, and with a very calm voice I told her, 'I have something else to do. Would you please excuse me?' And without giving her the usual kiss, I just walked away.

"By the time I reached the other side of the marketplace, I could feel her eyes on my shoulders. I did not want to turn my head, I don't know why. But finally, and very discreetly, I turned my head and saw them both still standing in the same place, watching my face.

"After a long walk, I ended up in a small bar, just to have a drink to calm myself, and to realize what had really happened to me and to her. Honestly, I still couldn't accept the truth; it seemed like a bad dream. Knowing her so well, I could not imagine even for a moment that she was capable of such a thing. I was not upset at all, but my mind was seized by a kind of paralysis.

"Many workers sat around the bar, drinking. There were also a few women. I did not want to hear about women, as I felt that women were a mystery. I had been going with Josephine seriously; I had dreamed of creating a family. I was not an adventurer. I had never betrayed Josephine even with a look. And at that time, every girl that I knew had been jealous of Josephine.

"One day, while I was still dating Josephine, I had been invited to a party. Josephine had also been invited, but she did not attend as she was sick. I was the only man without a partner, and that had provoked the thoughts of the daughter of a rich farmer, who approached me very politely and invited me to have a drink with her. I was not ready to accept her invitation, as I still hoped that Josephine could appear any minute. I did not want to give Josephine the smallest reason to be upset or to doubt my sincerity or my honesty. But this rich young girl was very persistent. When she finally realized that I wouldn't change my mind, she said, 'Do you really think that Josephine would behave in the same way as you do?' I was not happy to hear her remark, but I kept my expression impassive and chose not to react to her provocative remark. But even at that time, the slightest suspicion that Josephine might be with someone else did not enter my mind, and that evening had ended without Josephine or any other woman.

"I ordered a whiskey. Suddenly a very nice young girl came to my table. As usual, I wanted to ignore her presence, but there was something in her sad expression and eyes that I found arresting. She seemed helpless. She certainly did not look like a girl who was chasing a man. My mind was still occupied by Josephine, although I had given up all hope. But somehow, I couldn't keep myself from glancing at the girl's eyes. She didn't smile even for a moment. Her mind seemed to be preoccupied. She looked very concerned and said hesitantly, 'Young man, do you want a job on a farm?' At that time, I already had a job, but the word farm had attracted my attention. I looked at her for a moment, in order to see if her question was just an excuse to enter into conversation with me. She was silent and awaited my answer without insistence. I realized that she was serious, especially as she did not order even a single drink.

"I decided to answer with caution. 'Why me? There are so many men here.'

"She looked again at my eyes for a moment and continued, 'I need someone serious like you.' Her presence and her being instilled in me a feeling of calmness, trust and serenity. When Josephine had broken up with me, many thoughts had passed through my mind, and I had promised myself never to have anything to do with women again. It had been a shock. The young girl broke the silence again with, 'Would you like to work on a farm?' I did not really know what to answer; the idea of going to work on a farm appealed to me as the most appropriate thing to do, in order to forget Josephine. But I was hesitant to accept, as I was not sure if this was not another woman's trap. But I looked at her again, and realized that she was serious.

"I asked, 'Where?'

"She answered, 'On our farm.'

"'Why did your father send you to look for a man?'

"I did not realize that this question was extremely tactless, but she answered in a grave tone, 'My father is dead.' Her answer created in me a feeling of sorrow and pity. I knew that any further questions would be embarrassing to her. I answered, 'I am sorry, when can I start?' She stood up. 'Right now. Come with me before it gets too late. We shall travel in my coach.'

"I stood up and followed her without a second thought, not feeling the need to argue with her, as if I was being carried on a current. Outside, her coach and horse were waiting for us. We sat down next to each other, and the horse started off without even waiting for her command. I had a very strange feeling; I had just finished with Josephine and after less than an hour, here I was sitting with a girl whom I had never seen before, headed towards an unknown destination. At the same time, I felt I had known her for a long time. I asked her, 'What is your name?' 'Mary!' she answered. I suddenly felt at peace, because for me this name represented Saint Mary.

"I felt that my job had started already and asked her, 'Shall I drive?' Without hesitation and without a word she handed me the reins, and I continued to drive. We reached the farm after a three-hour ride. When we arrived, her mother was sitting outside awaiting her return. Her first remark was, 'Welcome home!' She did not seem to be in the best of health. Mary prepared a simple soup, and the three of us sat down around the table. I felt that I had found a home with a family.

"Mary left the table before us, and after a moment of absence she came back and said to me, 'Your bed is ready. We have to turn in early, as we have a long day ahead of us.'

"I couldn't sleep all night long. I thought of all that had happened to me within the span of less than a day. There had been a dramatic change in my life. Here I was, suddenly settled on a farm, with a family that I had never known before; but I never felt for a moment that they were strangers to me. I sensed a feeling of responsibility. Josephine was like a memory which receded with the distance.

"After a few months, Mary's mother passed away. All the neighboring farmers were present at the funeral. The priest did not cease for a moment from looking at me and at Mary. Mary did not have any family except for me, I thought. I had to be next to her; we must have looked like a married couple. Mary was a little confused with this situation. After the funeral services, the priest asked for my name. He kept looking at me. Then, in a fatherly tone, he said, 'Take care of Mary.' This remark was redundant. I thought he might have meant, 'don't abuse her' and found the thought very embarrassing.

"My behavior towards Mary had always been very proper; I had never had the slightest thought of having her as my wife. Later, all the people present at the funeral joined us at our farm for lunch. I looked at everyone warily;

I wanted to clarify our proper relation so they would not doubt my intentions. Then I hesitated, and thought it best to ignore them.

"The priest came to me while I was in the kitchen, to talk about Mary. I tried to avoid him, as I felt that this was not the right moment. But he did not give up and kept following me; finally, I faced him with 'Father, do you want to tell me something?'

"'Yes, my son, I wonder what we can do tonight.' At first, I did not understand his message, then I realized that he meant Mary and me; as we were strangers, we could not spend the night together in the same house. His concern disturbed me a lot. But I realized that he meant well for Mary, as her reputation and honor were at stake. He continued, 'I shall ask Mrs. Johnson if she is willing to sleep over at the farm, until we find a solution to your problem.'

"I was insulted, as I had never had the slightest thought about this. Before Mary's mother died, no one had paid any attention to me. Now, I had become a problem. I cared about Mary more than anyone else, but no one could sense my feelings. I found this ridiculous, especially on the first night after her mother's death, while Mary was obviously in distress.

The presence of Mrs. Johnson would not change anything anyway. If Mary and I wanted to be together, we could have done this even when her mother was alive. But I desisted, as I did not want to upset any traditions or cause any gossip. I cared more about Mary's honor than my own.

"A few days had already passed with Mrs. Johnson coming over to the farm. Mary was not as natural as she had been before. I could see in her look that she too was embarrassed, and she did not behave toward me the way she usually did.

"For the first time, I began to look at Mary in a different light. She was affable and kind. But I was compelled to hide my real feelings which I had discovered only recently; I knew now that Mary was very dear to me. I did not want to leave her, even for a moment. We exchanged few words and she seemed reticent to speak to me in front of Mrs. Johnson. Her look, however, became more and more expressive. I felt that she wanted to tell me something. Our relations had been limited to the exchange of looks. We spoke with our eyes.

"One day, when Mrs. Johnson was in the kitchen, I was going off to the field when Mary suddenly accompanied me to the door and held my hand. I felt a vibration pass through my entire being. I went to the field, but my mind did not stop for a moment from thinking about Mary and the warm touch of her hand. The work that I had accomplished before in an hour now took me all day, as I did not want to return and see Mrs. Johnson. I preferred to mull over the sensation that I had experienced, for the first time in my life, at the touch of Mary's hand.

"At that moment, I knew that I loved Mary more than anything in the world. I did not ask if Mary loved me too. I did not bother with such a question. Her hand told me everything. Now, I only wanted to touch her hand again and again. Mrs. Johnson's presence became a big obstacle.

"One day, I went to the neighboring church to see the priest. I told him about my feelings for Mary. He looked at me with a slight smile and said, 'Nothing wrong with this, my son. I understand you want to marry Mary.' Then he continued, 'I shall visit Mary and hope to be able to convince her. After all, you're a good fellow.' I felt relaxed, although I did not feel that he had to convince her. At least that was what I thought.

"I returned to the farm and felt my whole being tremble. The touch of her hand may have been just a friendly gesture. I was confused but decided not to think about it. If Mary chose to say no to the priest, I might have to leave the farm. Then I might never have the happiness of seeing her again. That thought saddened me even more. It had not been the same when I had left Josephine.

"I regretted having spoken to the priest, as I did not want to lose Mary. Between marrying her and losing her, I preferred to be content with the warm feeling of her hand and her presence.

"One day, while I was in the field, the priest paid a visit to Mary. I knew nothing about this. On my return, I was stupefied to see the priest waiting for me at the front door. I thought he wanted to break the news of Mary's refusal to me. I shook like a child. My steps slowed. I wanted to delay the receipt of any bad news. For a split second, I wanted to return to the field. Then the priest called out to me, 'Come, my son, I have good news for you.' I couldn't stop trembling. I was confused; I stood in front of the priest, not able to meet his eyes. I felt his eyes on me. Then he took my hand and said, 'Congratulations! I shall make arrangements for your wedding.' My heart raced at his words, but I did not know if it was from good luck or from joy. A few weeks later, your mother and I were wed."

THE SPIDER'S WEB

John looked at his father, his eyes brimming with admiration and love. For the first time, he saw what a kind and handsome man his father was. He did not stop watching him and was happy to hear the story of his father and mother. That night, he did not want to sleep alone in his bed. He hugged his father, who also felt affectionate and held his son tightly. This story had forged them both with love. John could sense the grace which bound them both, like mother and child.

Father and son shared the same bed till morning. The next day the sea was still calm. The sun shone. Neither of the men realized that they had slept till noon. Mr. de Montaigne seemed a little uneasy, as he had never opened his heart to anyone since his wife had died. He also felt relaxed and happy, as he had revived his best memories, which due to more pressing paternal obligations had had to be buried. He had never openly expressed to John anything about his love for his wife. Now John realized how much his father loved his mother. He felt sorry for his father and for himself, for he longed for her to see how much his father loved him. John had been too young to remember all the details about his mother, as he had to move to a different country and a new way of life. His father's struggle for their livelihood had preoccupied John more than anything else.

When Mr. de Montaigne went to lunch, John opted to stay in the cabin. His father's story had excited him. He looked for old pictures that his father had with him and finally found an old picture of his mother and grandmother. Both ladies stood next to the wells. He tried to feel his mother's love by looking at her eyes. He sensed a vibration and was amazed how the words from his father's story could transmit sensation from person to person. His feelings came alive and he had the impression that his mother was still alive. He felt that maybe he would find her again someday. But John did not want to dwell on this idea. He preferred to nurture the feeling that he found in his father's story and in the picture of his beloved mother.

He rushed to hide the photos before his father returned from lunch, as he did not want to show his feelings. From that day onwards, John treated his father with great love and care. He wished he could have been there at his grandmother's funeral, so that his father would not have had to suffer the presence of Mrs. Johnson. He could easily recall that place, as he still remembered his mother's farm. She had never told him anything about all this. Then he realized that his mother could not have talked to him about his father's love, as he had been a child at that time. Although he knew that he was young, such thoughts had emerged naturally. He felt he had to be a part of his parent's happiness. John had just replaced the picture when his father returned from lunch.

A fair wind had started to speed the ship along. In the late afternoon a stiff gale began to rock the vessel. John remembered the first night. He was immediately on the alert for his father. He felt sorry that his father had had lunch. He himself felt fine, as he had eaten nothing since the day before.

The captain seemed to be preoccupied with his crew. The passengers began to run to their cabins. As night approached, the movement of the vessel became more pronounced. John had already foreseen a rough night ahead. His only concern, however, was his father's health. Mr. de Montaigne seemed blissfully unaware of the turbulence. John's concern about the precautions he meant to take might have been premature, but he did not want to relax, even for a moment. He wanted to be prepared in case his father felt bad. The waves battered against the ship's side. Mr. de Montaigne seemed preoccupied. This time the revival of his love story had made him stronger. His thoughts followed the same pattern as John's. He took out his wife's picture and pressed it against his breast. John observed the scene with mixed feelings.

The storm did not seem to bother Mr. de Montaigne. The revival of old memories had made him look very young. John, meanwhile, went to the storeroom to fetch some towels. When he returned, his father was still holding the picture of his mother. John did not want to disturb him. During the night, his father slept like a child. John stayed awake the entire night as the vessel moved slowly and with a painful rhythm.

The next day, the sea was as calm as a pond, as if nothing had happened during the night. The dining room was in complete disarray, with bottles and broken china littering the floor. Once again Mr. de Montaigne went alone to take his breakfast, while John lay deep in slumber.

This was the second day that John had not eaten, and this time it was Mr. de Montaigne who was concerned about his son. He brought back a sandwich and a cup of tea with him. But John was still fast asleep, and his father did not want to disturb him.

He now had the opportunity to watch his son sleeping. John's face looked like that of his wife as she slept before her mother had died.

When John awoke, it was already noon. The sun shone brightly and there was not a trace of a wind. The sea reflected the shadow of the vessel as it sped along faster than the night before. John was glad to find a sandwich waiting for him and devoured it hungrily.

After finishing his tea and breakfast he smiled at his father in thanks. But he had another reason for smiling; he had dreamed about his mother. In the dream, he saw his father's wedding in the small church. He was certain this was not a dream but a vision. John continued to smile without saying anything to his father. The day passed quickly.

JOSEPHINE

Mr. de Montaigne asked John to dress well, as he wanted to dine with him and celebrate the revival of his happiness. John gladly accepted his father's invitation. Both gentlemen dressed in their best suits. The entry of this handsome couple caused many heads to turn in the dining room, and they were soon joined at the table by an old man accompanied by a young lady. The old man introduced himself as Mr. Moreland and he said, "My daughter, Josephine." John looked at his father with a hint of a smile. This was a rare coincidence, and John found it amusing. As the old man entertained Mr. de Montaigne, John felt that he had to entertain Josephine. His father's story was still fresh in his mind. During the conversation, he tried to associate her with his father's friend Josephine. He enjoyed her company, but he was careful not to be attracted to her, as her name was associated with a bad memory.

Josephine and John became traveling companions. Every day they promenaded from deck to deck. Mr. de Montaigne did not like the young lady. He associated her name with the character of his own Josephine. He did not want to express these thoughts to John. John, on his side, felt the same way, but he did not want to be unjust to Josephine. In any case, she was a passenger like him, and if she could make the voyage more agreeable, there was no problem, so he thought. After all, she was from another generation. He could now understand why people sometimes had a prejudice against one another, often without reason, as in the case of Josephine.

But they grew to like each other more every day. Mr. de Montaigne observed the development of this relationship with skepticism. He liked her as a lady for her education and breeding. She always treated him with respect. She had no idea about their thoughts and Mr. de Montaigne's story. Her father was a highly respected man, somewhat old to have Josephine as a daughter.

Mr. de Montaigne limited his conversation with the father to business. He was a rich man from the United States. He had spent a year with his daughter in Europe before embarking on the vessel to India. He supposedly had a large company in the United States, as well as plantations in India. This much Mr. de Montaigne had extracted from the various conversations that he had had with him.

John was attracted to Josephine, not by her father's wealth, but by her personality. She was a very charming young woman and close to John's age. John never tried to enter into any discussion about the United States or personal matters. Their main subjects of conversation were literature and history.

One evening, they were both on deck. The sea was calm and reflected the light of the full moon. The atmosphere was right for romance. John felt like kissing her, but somehow his father's story dampened his ardor and he stopped himself from going any further. That night, Josephine had been ready to kiss John. She waited. Nothing happened. Josephine could not understand John. She thought maybe he was being prudent and did not want to take the risk of being refused. She knew, though, that John was attracted by her charm. She loved him. She decided to be patient. After all, the trip was a long one, and surely the occasion would present itself on another night.

Mr. Moreland liked John very much, and the thought of having him for a son-in-law did not displease him. He played in his mind with the idea. During the long voyage, he made the

THE SPIDER'S WEB

effort to be nice to Mr. de Montaigne. He saw him as a future member of his family, with whom he would spend a lot of time in India.

Mr. de Montaigne was growing impatient; the trip seemed endless to him. He wished the ship would bring them as soon as possible to their destination, so that John would end his romance with Josephine. He did not want to show his feelings to John, as he did not want to appear unfair to Josephine.

The vessel had become their home away from home. Every day passed pleasantly. The sea became a part of them. Mr. de Montaigne's story about his Josephine became a burden to John, for he liked Josephine Moreland. He had become accustomed to her and enjoyed her company very much. Her presence gave him an agreeable feeling. He could not see himself now travelling without her. For a long time, the de Montaignes had not experienced the presence of women, and Josephine had now become a part of their daily lives. It was something new to them both.

Mr. de Montaigne was very reserved about this young lady. The name Josephine awoke sad memories in him. He did not want to appear insensitive towards John, but John's feelings towards Josephine were becoming a matter of concern to him. He continued to be polite towards the young lady and towards his son.

Josephine was as attractive as she was intelligent and charming. Mr. Moreland was very pleased to have a young gentleman like John at his side. He liked him very much. For the first time, he experienced the feeling of being in a family. Josephine had taken on the new role very seriously and looked after her father and both John and his father. Everything seemed to be in harmony. Mr. de Montaigne had also found a rich new friend. This might very well help to resolve all his problems in the new land.

One evening, while John and Josephine were alone on deck, looking out at the sea, the two older gentlemen were on the opposite side of the vessel exchanging business stories.

John loved Josephine but had abstained from revealing his feelings to her. His father's story about the older Josephine and John's mother had already disturbed his feelings. But that story was not the only one he knew. John, as he watched the sea merge into the horizon, recalled his first trip to London. At that time his father had had to work during school vacations. Not wishing to deprive his son of new experiences, he had sent him to spend a few weeks with one of his friends, who was the captain of a ship and was married with two children.

John was almost seventeen at the time, and the trip had left him with a very bad memory. The experience of Mrs. Martin now acted as a warning. He could not forget the story of Mrs. Martin, who had been old at that time and seemed to be a respectable lady despite her experiences.

He had boarded the train and found himself with Mrs. Martin, with whom he shared the compartment. She introduced herself politely and seemed eager to converse with him. Though only seventeen, he looked older than his years. The suffering that he had endured with his father had given him a serious and conscientious air.

When the train began to move, John was very happy and eager to meet other people. He stood next to the window to watch the landscape. The train gathered speed. He felt the momentum as he watched the telegraph poles whir past. He was silent and absorbed by this new journey. The old lady had addressed a few words to him, but he was embarrassed for not having understood her. Wishing to appear polite, he sat down next to her. He still could not understand what she was saying, what with the noise from the train and from the open window.

He prepared himself to listen attentively to her. This behavior did not go unnoticed by Mrs. Martin, who had been discreetly admiring his charm and cultivated appearance. John's presence had revived many forgotten memories in her, and now she had an occasion to share them with John.

"Is this your first trip, young man?" she enquired. John, who wanted to be kind, did not feel it necessary, however, to answer such a direct question. After all, he did not want to show that he was an inexperienced young man. Usually he traveled with his father. He did not know what to reply without giving her question considerable thought, as his father had always taught him. So he remained silent. Mrs. Martin realized that her question would not receive any answer from John. She did not insist, and went on with another remark.

"I always liked to travel when I was young, but I never had the opportunity." John, relieved from the first question, felt that this statement deserved a polite rejoinder and said, without losing time,

"I hope you do not have any feelings of regret, madam, now that you are able to travel." He felt that it was his duty to comfort this old lady, who could have been his grandmother, and without waiting for an answer he continued, "I like traveling; it offers many new experiences and adventures."

Mrs. Martin, upon hearing the words "experiences" and "adventures", immediately took to her role as an old lady and said with a smile, "Adventures! That was how I met my husband for the first time. I was young and innocent then, and eager to meet a young man. I did not know my husband well enough, but I was happy to be courted. When we had known each other even less than a month, he wanted to marry me. I was proud when he asked for my hand. I accepted without hesitation and without the consent of my parents, or their advice. I could not imagine then that a marriage was such a serious commitment. My only concern and preoccupation at that time was to have a man. In those days, that was the concern of every young lady. We did not have so many opportunities to meet young men; men are lucky."

John listened to Mrs. Martin patiently. Although he had never met a young lady, he did not want to contradict her. He preferred to let her believe that he was lucky. He had never had a conversation with an old lady before, as he had not known his grandmother. This was his first experience of this kind. He noticed her eyes, which were still lively and youthful, and tried to imagine how she had looked when she was young. As he was looking at her, she continued,

"Young man!"

"My name is John."

"John! Are you visiting a friend in London?"

"Yes, madam."

"I was proud to be betrothed. We then married and we even had a daughter."

John replied, "Madam, you must have been happy."

On hearing the word "happy", she grimaced.

"I cannot complain now, it is too late."

John, who was shocked to hear this, enquired, "Why is it late, madam?"

"Oh! It is a long story," answered Mrs. Martin, with a resigned wave of her hand. She went on, "Why not? After all, it was an extraordinary experience. So you want to hear my story?"

John, not wishing to embarrass the old lady, smiled. Mrs. Martin took it to mean that John had no objection and continued, "I realized a month later that I liked my husband, who was ideal in every respect, but somehow I missed something. He was not jealous at all. Or so I thought! One day, as I was talking to my friend Pierre, my husband appeared suddenly with a surly expression on his face. I realized that he was jealous. I interrupted my conversation with Pierre and gave my husband a kiss and we went directly home. On the way, he was silent. When we reached home, he made a scene and told me that he did not want me to be seen with any other man; later, he apologized for his behavior and explained that he did not want to lose me.

"Pierre had been my lover long before I knew my husband. He was not an easy man, though. He loved me in his way, but he never wanted to marry me. At this juncture, I realized that I had to end my relationship with Pierre who, on hearing my decision, made a big to-do. To keep the peace, I continued my life between my husband and Pierre.

"It was not easy. My life became more complicated from day to day, as I had to lie and create new stories. My life turned into a farce. However, I managed without having to hurt either of them. Except for one night. It was pouring with rain outside. I lay in Pierre's bed, too lazy to get up and go home. You know how it is when you are in a warm bed?"

John, who had never heard a story like this from his father, was looking at Mrs. Martin with eagerness and astonishment. "When I finally decided to go home, it was two o'clock in the morning. I was very nervous and could not think of any story or excuse with which to placate my husband. I prayed he would be asleep, so that I could enter silently. To my disappointment, my husband was awake and waiting for me in the living room. When I saw his face, I was scared that this time it was the end of my acting and of my life. I felt sorry for him, for he did not deserve such treatment from me. After all, I was his wife, and he had always been very good to me at all times. It was my fault. I hated disappointing anyone. Now I saw my life ending in disgrace and tragedy and scandal."

John was listening avidly to the story and tried to put himself in her husband's place. He could imagine what happened and did not want to hear the end of the story, thinking that it must have ended in tragedy. He interrupted Mrs. Martin, "Did you love your husband?"

Mrs. Martin, who wanted to finish her narrative, did not answer and continued, "I knew that that was the end. I steeled myself, smiled at my husband and took off my coat, when suddenly the terrifying voice of my husband shook my entire being, 'Where were you, for God's sake?'

"I thought that my husband had worked out everything, and any more lies would only provoke him further. I decided to tell him the truth and replied, 'I was with my lover.' He looked at me. Then he smiled, as though he preferred to ignore the truth. He hugged me and kissed me and took me to bed. That night I was really tired and racked with emotion. To have two men in the same night was too much!"

John interrupted her, "That's it? He did not question you any further?"

"No," replied Mrs. Martin. "He apologized for having raised his voice. Men do not like to hear the truth, especially when you serve the truth directly and without embellishment. They prefer not to accept the truth rather than face a hard choice."

John, feeling that he had to make an intelligent reply, rejoined, "It is not always agreeable to hear the truth, which can change our lives entirely. We prefer to live with our lies and comedy rather than face reality. As I understand it, madam, your husband preferred to believe that it was a joke."

"Yes, young man, you understand why it

is terrible to betray a husband. For the sake of peace and my daughter, my life became even more complicated, as I met a third man, one I really loved."

"What about your husband and Pierre?" interrupted John.

"I did not love either of them, but I had to preserve my family, especially my daughter, so I sacrificed my life for her. Have you any idea what it is to spend fifteen years with three men?"

John was so taken aback by the old lady's story that he felt like a little boy who does not know his way to school. He was a little afraid; his dreams and hopes were shaken by the interesting but sad story of this lady, who did not seem to be unhappy on the one hand, but seemed to feel sorry for herself on the other. John was very keen to hear the end of the story but was interrupted by the train coming to a halt at a station. More passengers entered their compartment, and the old lady realized that she couldn't continue with her story. She bent forward discreetly and whispered in John's ear, so that no one could hear,

"My son, my life is too long. My name is Mrs. Martin." And so ended the story of Mrs. Martin, which left an indelible impression on

John's mind. Now, recalling the story of Mrs. Martin, he forgot all about the story of Josephine. But Mr. de Montaigne never knew Mrs. Martin's story which for John was more dramatic than that of his father. Somehow, Josephine's story and Mrs. Martin's story became confused in John's mind and became one story.

John thought about Mrs. Martin as he watched Josephine. She did not know what was going on in his mind and looked at him and said, "John, do you love me?" John was perplexed. He did not want to answer her question, as he was not ready to express his feelings. He dreamed about an ideal marriage, with love, devotion and loyalty. But he said nothing. He did not want to answer in a way that might change his entire life before being sure that he had chosen the right woman.

He knew that he loved Josephine, but he was still under the influence of Josephine's and Mrs. Martin's stories. He hesitated. He did not want to compromise anyone. He preferred to wait, as Mrs. Martin had suggested, until he found his life's companion. On the other hand, John did not want to lose Josephine, as she could very well be the person he was looking for.

Josephine, seeing that John was not reacting

to her questions, hugged him suddenly and kissed him on the lips. This made him even more confused. He felt that he loved her, but he would never have taken the initiative to kiss Josephine. Now, a romance started between them, despite John's resistance and hesitation. Josephine was too young to be married, even if John had so wanted. He did not want to be like the husband of Mrs. Martin. He would rather take the risk of continuing to seem indifferent and to wait and see. They still had another week to go until they reached India.

Meanwhile, Mr. de Montaigne had had a long discussion with his new friend Mr. Moreland. They came over to the young couple to announce that it was time for dinner. John was happy to be interrupted, as he wanted to change the subject with Josephine, and the arrival of his father was a welcome excuse to interrupt his confusion and put a stop to this new situation.

When all four friends were in the dining room, Josephine tried to get John to talk. She changed her tone, but John's mind was deep in another story. Josephine's kiss was not the first kiss which he had not initiated.

When he had been the captain's guest in London, he had had a similar experience. The captain had been waiting for him at the station on the first day and had greeted him with a warm hello. Then they had taken a coach home.

When John arrived at his host's home, he was received by a charming lady. This was Olivia Green, the captain's wife. John was very shy. He hastened to give her the present that his father had bought for her. Mr. Green, who had to go somewhere, left John with Olivia, and said to her, "Olivia, take care of our young friend. Show him our English hospitality."

Olivia waved to her husband and closed the door. In an effort to make John, who was laboring under so many different impressions, feel at home, Olivia took his hand to show him around the house. The soft touch of Olivia's hand sent a current vibrating through his entire body. Olivia, without a second thought, kissed him on the mouth. John did not offer any resistance. By now, John felt as if he was in a dream. This was his first physical contact with a woman. After that incident, Olivia did not leave him in peace. She cherished him like a son and a lover at the same time.

When the captain returned home in the evening, John felt quite embarrassed. Every time the captain looked at him, he had the impression that the captain had guessed something. But Mr. Green had not an inkling of what was going through John's mind. His wife loved him so much, he had no reason to doubt her fidelity, and John was very young. Olivia, as she served dinner, kept teasing John, who did not know where to put himself.

The stories of John's father, Mrs. Martin, and Olivia were juxtaposed in John's mind. Josephine, believing that John was really in love with her, kept up a lively flow of conversation, so as not to attract the attention of the older gentlemen, who were enjoying the meal and their own discussion.

The thought of marriage was far from John's mind, especially after all the painful experiences that his father and he had had. To him, a woman was a creature that he would love to love but not with whom he could build a family. John wondered if there was any normal family in the world. His sole dream was of India, where he might discover another truth.

Throughout the rest of the voyage, he tried to avoid Josephine's advances, without appearing impolite or unkind. He had always tried to be dignified and reserved. This attitude attracted Josephine even more. She dreamed about his allure. John had replaced her father as Josephine's primary concern. John's father had not noticed anything special in his demeanor through the entire journey.

Early one morning, in the misty light of dawn, the western coastline was sighted. The vessel gradually slowed down as the Indian shoreline drew nearer. John's delight knew no bounds. With his natural inquisitiveness, he had discovered that this ship was about to dock at Ballard Pier, one of the numerous docks of Bombay harbor. To his left, he would see a magnificent arch, the Gateway of India, built by the British to honor Queen Victoria.

The ship laboriously maneuvered its way between other ships anchored in the Bombay harbor, along the wooden pier. Some vessels were still loading bulks of tea. Others were unloading various types of merchandise coming to India from England or the Netherlands. Flags of innumerable nations fluttered on the masts of the various ships. The vessels reverberated with the loud multilingual voices of sailors from every corner of the globe.

For the first time, John saw dark-skinned Indians, heads wrapped in colorful turbans, busy at work on the pier. Short, stocky coolies, clad in the blue uniforms of the docks, unloaded heavy bales of merchandise with practiced ease. Interspersed with the natives were the English policemen and soldiers, checking all kinds of official papers. John was amazed to see the milling crowds. He had never seen so many people at one time in his life. One could get lost among so many people, he murmured to himself. He could never have guessed how different this country was from any he had seen on the European continent. He realized for the first time that despite the numerous languages and dialects, English was the official language and he felt glad he knew English.

The vessel took almost half a day to come to a standstill. It was almost noon. John, eager not to miss a thing, had even neglected to eat breakfast. Now, a few Englishmen in uniform came on board. John could not distinguish between the soldiers and the policemen, as they were all dressed in short-sleeved shirts and shorts, with the round hats, or *topis*, as they were called. Mr. de Montaigne was busy with the luggage. Too late, John realized that he should have helped his father. But this new world was so full of distractions. When he finally reached his father, the trunks had already been dispatched.

John remembered that he had broken a promise to himself to take care of his father, and here he was absorbed by the spectacle like a child.

He could see Josephine and her father, at a distance, on deck, but chose to stay with his father. His heart quickened at the thought of seeing Josephine before they disembarked, as he had not even asked her for her address. He realized that he had forgotten something, but his mind was confused. Suddenly, he felt a touch on his shoulder. It was Josephine, who came to bid him farewell. He looked at her tongue-tied, but with so much to say. He wished he had had another day with her, just to be near her. Now, everything seemed lost.

With much hesitation, he gathered courage and said, "Josephine, you never told me where I could reach you."

Josephine, pretty in her summer hat, smiled and announced complacently, "Your father knows where to reach us." When he heard that his father knew Josephine's address, he was embarrassed, as he realized that his father had been thinking of Josephine. He smiled to hide his thoughts and said,

"Very well. I shall see you later." Josephine joined her father, who was waiting for her.

John was impatient going through the checkpoint, with all the time-consuming procedure of customs. Mr. de Montaigne, realizing that John had not had breakfast and must be tired and hungry, decided he must do something. He exchanged a few words with an Indian policeman, and suddenly they were hurried through.

INDIA

Europe now seemed so far away that John doubted he would ever return. The long voyage had been pleasant but exhausting. Now, as he stood on the pier, he felt the ground heave under him. The continuous clamoring of different tongues, the bustling passengers, and the continuous motion of the ship, had weakened him. He started to dream about a real bed, just for a bit of rest. Everything he was seeing merged in a whirl of black. He wondered why he had not anticipated such a different world. Meanwhile, his father, struggling to get his belongings safely off the pier, waved to him to indicate that all was well.

When John and his father finally emerged outside, Mr. Mershenson was waiting for them. John did not recognize him at first, but when his father hugged him, he realized it was their old friend from Paris. John, who had begun to feel lost and low-spirited, suddenly felt reassured.

Mr. Mershenson, who had become a very rich and respected individual, had arranged for his large and well-appointed carriage to pick them up at the exit from the pier.

John could not think any more about all the dreams he had regarding India. The only thing he wanted was to get out of this densely populated city, where he could not walk a step without rubbing shoulders with someone, and which was so different from Paris and London. He had given up trying to watch anything. He was entirely disinterested. Getting away was his only thought.

John had a strange sense of displacement in this new world. He remembered having the same feeling when he arrived in Paris for the first time. Nor had the kind Mr. Mershenson recognized him, either, for he now looked like a man, except that his emotions were still like those of a child. He was still very impressionable.

Mr. de Montaigne took his place on the left side of the coach, while John sat in the middle, squeezed in between his father and Mr. Mershenson. His thoughts were now no longer directed to a bed, but to the rhythm of the wheels which had begun to roll. He could not imagine coming to this land if his father were not with him. Mr. Mershenson's benign presence was a comfort. John did not ask how far they had to go.

Mr. Mershenson had come a long way to receive his friend; his residence was about fifty miles from Bombay. John hoped that the trip would not last long, and even if he had to suffer for an hour, he would recuperate from the fatigue and malaise of being wedged between the two portly gentlemen, who had not desisted from incessant discussion as they updated each other on all the news.

John had lost the thread of the conversation, his mind occupied by his legs, which were becoming more and more numb. He did not want to interrupt his father just to tell him how uncomfortable he was. The two elderly gentlemen had no idea that John was in such discomfort. He did not know what to do. He tried to concentrate his mind on something else, but every time he turned to look at the landscape, he saw his father's face on one side and Mr. Mershenson's on the other.

It was almost five o'clock in the afternoon, and now his mind had shifted to Josephine. He wondered where she might be at this hour and how far she might be from him. Then his mind wandered to Josephine's father, then to Mrs. Martin, and finally to Olivia.

He realized that every human being has an

inner world, as well as an outer world for society. John understood that it was not sufficient to know someone from the outside. This thought saddened him. He had simply not been aware of the unwritten rules and conventions of society. He realized that Josephine, who attracted him so much with her charm, her attitude, her looks, and her behavior, could be displaying only one side of her character, the social side. He also realized that he did not know her well enough to make a long-term commitment to her. If only he could penetrate her heart and her mind, all his problems would be resolved in a trice.

John was now so deep in thought that he was unaware of the motion of the coach and did not notice the pain in his legs any more. His mind was rapt in a question to which he had no answer: "Was Josephine just pretending to be a nice person?" She actually had never spoken about herself, her childhood or her mother. He could not understand how he could have been with her so long on the ship without asking her any question which might have resolved this quandary which was now weighing heavily on his heart and mind.

He wondered if everyone waited until they were older before telling the real story of their life, like Mrs. Martin, who had divulged to him the story of her life, or maybe only a part of it? She seemed to have talked frankly, but he wondered why she had shared with him, a total stranger, the most confidential story of her life? Maybe because she was old and had nothing to lose, or maybe she wanted to revive some vestige of her youth, when she was still pure and innocent. She was now a grandmother and probably had to be there for her grandchildren, but she also had to live with a past which she could never erase from her memory.

Mrs. Martin seemed to have so much on her heart and mind, memories of all kinds, full of pain, and misery, and happiness. She carried a secret pain that seemed to reach down to her very soul. John realized the courage of a mother who went through her daily obligations, her love and concern for her children, despite the experiences of her youth.

We think that our life on earth is infinite, but in reality we are not aware of what we have. The only capital we have is time. Everyone has at his disposal a finite amount of time. If we only knew exactly how much time we had at our disposal!

It dawned on John that time is the most precious thing a human being can have, like a jar of water in the desert, which dwindles from day to day and from hour to hour. Our life span is reduced with every drop we consume. John regretted not having used his time more wisely.

John had never seen a desert, but now a desert appeared vividly in his mind. He realized that we take our life for granted and fritter away our time without concern. He could not conceive how a human being could survive alone in a desert with the knowledge that the quantity of water he possessed would determine how long he lived. He began to comprehend why society, with all that is good and bad, is indispensable to the existence of humanity. Water and food are ties that unite people, despite our different opinions about each other. These ties are the lifeblood that we all share, like the air that we all share without dispute.

The air that penetrates deep into our lungs and blood is the most generous denominator. If only the air could speak, it could tell us about our neighbor and friend, as it is the only element that seeps through us all and without our permission nourishes the minutest cells of our whole being. Air is the only omnipresent element that everyone not only allows to penetrate their privacy, but that everyone is eager to have.

John suddenly felt the coach slow down. He came back to the present without realizing that he had traveled for many hours without feeling the pain of the trip. He glanced out the window, but it was already dark.

Throughout the entire trip the two elderly gentlemen had been so absorbed in their conversation that they had been completely oblivious to John's presence. John had not paid any attention to their stories; he had been far too absorbed in his own plight. On board ship, he had at least been able to move his legs freely. Mr. Mershenson and his father were rather heavily built compared to the slender John.

Suddenly his father noticed him and inquired solicitously, "Are you all right, my son? We are here at last!"

John, who was embarrassed by this question, simply replied, "Yes." His father had no idea that the trip had been such a terrible experience for him. His father's spirits were soaring at seeing his best friend again, and John did not want to dampen them. All he wanted was to get out of the coach and walk. This had been an exceptional and excruciating experience.

THE ESTATE

The carriage had pulled up at the impressive front door of a beautiful mansion. Mr. Mershenson alighted, then John stepped down, and his father after him. A very well-dressed butler stood at the front door. Two Indian helpers took care of the luggage. John felt relieved just to breathe deeply of the pure air and to be able to move his legs. His father did not seem tired at all.

Mr. Mershenson glanced at his watch and said, "We are on time. I told you I did not live far. You see we made it in four and a half hours. Isn't that just marvellous!" John kept his less than enthusiastic opinion to himself. Mr. Mershenson, with a grand gesture, said, "Gentlemen, consider this your home!" John paid no heed to Mr. Mershenson. He was busy getting the circulation in his legs going again.

John finally began to get over the ordeal of the coach trip. The butler politely said, "Gentlemen, will you please follow me." John turned back for a last look at the coach, then followed the butler, who led them to a very large room. "Mr. de Montaigne, this is your room," he said. The room opened to a large bedroom, which was part of a spacious suite. He then ambled over toward a high-ceilinged corridor, with wide-open windows and a floor checkered with black and white marble tiles.

Everything appeared to be meticulously clean. John, without a word, followed the butler. Several doors opened out at the end of the corridor. The butler, in his clipped accent, said to him, "Sir, your room is to the left." He opened the door to let John in and said, "I shall be back for you in one hour." John was overwhelmed with his surroundings and the impressive butler.

He entered his room and, after closing the door, bounced on the soft bed like a child. It was large and comfortable. Without taking his clothes off, thoroughly exhausted, he was soon sound asleep.

The butler had been with Mr. Mershenson since the time he lived in London. He was now older and grayer, but impressive nonetheless. In London the butler did not have such a big house to take care of. He had heard of John and his father but had never met them. Mr. Mershenson could not then have afforded a butler, but this man had worked for Mr. Mershenson's father, who had been wealthy.

Mr. Mershenson, despite tightened straits in London, had been unwilling to give up his butler, especially after he lost his wife.

Before his death, Mr. Mershenson's father had given the butler a few words of advice, "My son, stay loyal to whoever you work for and remember, it is a greatness to be of service." The butler never forgot these words. He went through trials and tribulations with Mr. Mershenson when the latter's financial situation was precarious. And now he realized the wisdom of his old master. As Mr. Mershenson became richer, the butler remembered his old master's words, "Enjoy your job and don't envy the fortune of others. It is better to have a fortunate master than to be fortunate oneself. As a butler, you will enjoy your master's riches more than your master will. It is not important what you possess, but what you do." The wise advice of the old master became a reality for the butler.

John awoke after less than half an hour. He was thrilled to see his dream turning to reality. He realized that it was time he got dressed, as the butler would soon be there to pick him up, probably for dinner. He would much rather have relaxed and not dressed. He looked out at the sky through the window. Everything seemed like a dream. The stars did not have the same color as the stars that he had seen from the ship. But here through the wide-open window, the sky looked like a large painting. On the right hand side of the room was an old English-style commode. Above the commode hung a bamboo-framed wall mirror. John noticed that the bamboo style did not match the rest of the English-styled pieces.

He looked at his face in the mirror and realized that something in him had changed, especially in the expression of the eyes. He attributed this change to fatigue. He could not remember his father's room, but by now time was running, and he still had to wash himself and get dressed. He had not finished putting on his socks when he heard the slow tread of the butler in the corridor. He quickly put on his tie and jacket, took a last look in the mirror and saw that his hair was still disheveled. He looked for his hair brush in vain, then ran his fingers through his hair and heard the butler knock on the door.

He followed the butler leisurely. This time John looked more refined than when he had arrived. He could not understand why the butler was walking so slowly, but he noticed that his pace was measured and as precise as clockwork.

He then stopped in front of another door and knocked. This was John's father's room. "Will you please follow me to the dining room," said the butler. John was now told that they were about to dine. His father was dressed in his best suit that he had worn on board ship.

John wished that he had dressed in his best suit too. Then he remembered what his father had once said to him, "It is not important what you put in your mouth, but what comes out of it. No one sees what you have in your stomach, but people do notice how you are dressed." John did not understand what his father had meant and felt vaguely uneasy for not having taken in his father's lesson.

The butler led the way to the living room, where Mr. Mershenson, dressed impeccably, was sitting on a sofa. When John and his father entered, he received them with much warmth and gladness, as in the old days. This time, the two older gentlemen looked alike in their suits.

"So, gentlemen, have you recovered from your trip?" asked Mr. Mershenson.

Mr. de Montaigne answered with his suave smile, "The room is perfect, and I am very comfortable, thank you."

"And you, John?" continued Mershenson.

THE SPIDER'S WEB

John, typically embarrassed, hesitated then said, "I certainly could use some more sleep. The bed is so soft."

Mr. Mershenson did not wait for John's answer. In any case, John did not really know what to reply. A response was a mere formality, even if it was redundant or not necessarily truthful. In such circumstances, people are used to making small talk without sense or meaning, as a way to entertain guests. Such questions and remarks were new for John. He knew that from now on he had to get used to this new way of life, which was characteristic of English-speaking countries.

While the two older gentlemen talked for a while, the butler appeared a second time to announce that dinner was ready. John felt relieved, as he had been trying to entertain himself by admiring a painting that hung on a wall. The living room was immense in comparison to what he was used to. When he had entered the dining room, he had been shocked by the size of the dining table, which was more than twelve feet long. Mr. Mershenson placed his father at one end and sat down at the head of the table. John had the choice of taking any of a dozen chairs, but the butler had already prepared a place for him. All these changes had happened within the same day... from the small ship cabin to the crowded pier teeming with people, to the sumptuous dining just for three people.

The butler stood by during the entire dinner, ready for any indication from Mr. Mershenson. The two gentlemen did not cease to exchange views and anecdotes from past experiences. John was silent all along. The dinner was delicious and elegantly served. They had rice pulao, savory with spices and turkey. The meal would have amply sufficed for an entire family. They partook only of small portions. John understood the strong Western influence and found it disturbing in comparison with the Oriental.

He wondered if he would have to spend long periods alone and silent, since the two gentlemen were always so preoccupied with each other. The estate was so large that a hundred people could get lost in it. He wondered why Mr. Mershenson needed such a large house. He recalled that Mr. Mershenson had a daughter, but refrained from asking after her, since a long time had elapsed since they lived in Paris and many things could have come to pass.

John wondered about the daughter, whom he could not recall having ever met but only having heard about from Mr. Mershenson. The ceremonious dinner finally came to an end, and it was already late for their first day after the journey. John was tired and his eyes began to close by themselves. He could have kept himself awake, but he had never longed as much for a bed as on this evening.

When Mr. Mershenson finally stood up, John was overwhelmed with relief. Mr. Mershenson walked them out of the room and remarked, "I hope you will sleep well under my roof. Get a good night's rest and tomorrow we will visit the entire estate and wheat fields."

John listened to Mr. Mershenson with joy and curiosity and remained politely silent. Society has its rules and conventions. Even if he thought differently, he knew he should keep his thoughts to himself. He went on to his room. He could not fall asleep, as he had so many conflicting thoughts and emotions in his mind from this extraordinary first day. He passed the time hanging up his clothes and placing the books that he had brought from Europe on the shelves. This was the first night that he had had to spend by himself ever since he was a boy, and he missed his father's stories. This first night was a prelude to an era that John had dreamed about for a long time. It was dark outside and John could see nothing outside the window.

This sensation of being alone was entirely new for John. He now digested the awesome silence and independence. The room was large and John paced about. He lay awake late into the night, eagerly awaiting the arrival of dawn. He promised himself that he would not miss the sunrise. But the elegant dinner and the majestic house had impressed him a great deal and his mind teemed with thoughts about the civilization and the culture of this new place. He had thought before that he had discovered to a large extent what society was like. Now it became clear to him that he was still far from knowing what life was all about, and about the various influences around us, with or without our conscious knowledge. The more he thought he knew something, the more he realized that he knew nothing. Life was even more mysterious than he had imagined.

The first day came, and despite his fatigue the bright Asian sun awakened him. He jumped up to look out the window at the landscape. He discovered all kinds of flowers that he had never seen before. The bright sun had given him clarity which was completely new to him.

He now began to question all he had seen until then. He wondered if this was the paradise that his father had spoken of before. In Europe, he could not have imagined that the light of the sun could be brighter. Now the daylight made his heart overflow with joy. Was this brightness the last phase, or was there another brightness that he still had to discover?

John thought of the acute hearing of dogs that can hear sounds in wavelengths that are inaudible to human ears, about the various forces in physics that he had been taught and that we are aware of but cannot see. How many things are still to be discovered that exist already and that we are not aware of! Life was a mystery that would unfold by itself.

He also understood that he had to keep these thoughts to himself. He knew no one he could share them with. He sensed that we are all like a flock of sheep led by a shepherd. None of the lambs would wander off, for fear of getting lost. Yet fear was the barrier to many good things in life that we could eventually discover in ourselves. Fear is both our weakness and our strongest enemy. Fear reduces us to nothing. John began to understand that he had first to overcome the fear within himself which held him back. He had to face it and overcome it.

All these thoughts had never occurred to him when he was in Europe or on the ship. He could not imagine that he had been only one night on the Asian continent. He sensed a change in himself which made him more alive and aware of every detail and sensation. Every flower seemed to talk to him with its blooming fragrance and beauty. The new colors were a true discovery; until then he had never thought of the existence of new colors. The beauty of an orchid amazed him. He saw himself transplanted to a new world which he had only just begun to discover. The long journey by ship now seemed like a faded dream.

After the English breakfast, the three gentlemen set out on a walk. This time everyone was dressed in colonial style, with cork hats to protect them from the strong sunlight. Mr. Mershenson had a walking stick and went ahead, explaining everything in sight to his friend, Mr. de Montaigne. Old habits die hard, and soon their conversation had turned to business. John was annoyed by this and walked a few paces behind to avoid their conversation. He wondered how all his delightful discoveries could pass unnoticed by his father. The men seemed to have time only to talk about business. He felt sorry for his father, at his inability to enjoy the landscape, the new sensations, and the beauty all around them.

This new land meant more to John than business and wheat. It signified revival, hope, new light, new colors, new people, and a different air to breathe from the old air of Europe. He enjoyed the walk. He was absorbed by the fields of wheat, rippling with every breeze like waves in a pond. The greens were a deeper, darker hue than he had ever seen. Mr. de Montaigne and his friend had gained distance, and John was now far behind. He enjoyed every step, drank in every sunbeam through his pores. His face and body radiated a new vigor. He wished this walk would last forever.

His pace gradually slowed down as he watched the strong, supple, bronze-skinned women busy harvesting the ripened grain and cutting off the sheaves with a sharp sickle in an age-old movement that he had never seen before. The skin tone was new to him and held a special charm, quite different from the deliberately cultivated charm of European women. The women worked silently, like honey bees, each one adept in her place and action. They were busy and did not ask questions or talk to one another. They looked like they were part of the wheat fields themselves.

In the distance, he could see some women threshing the sheaves to separate the grain. They then poured the grain and husk into large woven straw baskets which they flung into the air to separate the grain from the chaff. John marveled at all the work that was done manually, but for these simple villagers it was the only life they knew.

Here was a world entirely new: new people, new colors. We believe that we know all the colors in the world, only to discover a new tint, a new shade. John thought about all the basic colors that he had learnt in school. He was now inclined to believe that our eyes have been adapted to see what we want them to see or what we are able to see. This ability was now slowly changing and letting him discover other ways, other colors. How many things had our eyes not yet discovered in life? The more educated and sophisticated we are, the more we believe that we know more than those who are not impinged by "civilization".

In reality we know too little about nature and about ourselves. John had come all the way to Asia to discover new flowers, new colors, new skin tones and a brightness that his eyes had never before beheld. Now, he began to look back in his mind. His studies, his school, his teacher, everyone and everything had been smart, but this new reality had completely overwhelmed the past and opened the way to the future.

John again thought about the dogs that hear sounds inaudible to human ears. He reasoned that what is not accessible to us does not necessarily not exist. This little example threw off balance all the old concepts that he had spent his entire youth learning. John now began to think of other ways to see and understand life. Mr. de Montaigne and Mr. Mershenson were almost forgotten as they moved in the distance like a pair of shadows.

John stood looking at the two figures as they disappeared over the horizon. "It is strange," he murmured to himself, "how our sight loses precision over distance." The two gentlemen had become almost insignificant. One could say they did not exist. John knew for certain that his father and Mr. Mershenson were not visible to him, but that they existed. This thought confirmed to him that our sight is relatively good but not perfect. One could say the same for our hearing. If John did not already know that his father and Mr. Mershenson were walking, he could have pretended that they did not exist.

John concluded from this little example that it could be that we are not aware of all kinds of existence. What we do not see and do not hear may not be nonexistent. This thought persisted. There must be other kinds of life that our eyes are not able to see, like physical forces, which though invisible, exist. He wished he had other senses or abilities which would enable him to see any other type of life, sound or color that share this planet with us. He was quite convinced by these thoughts relating to the disappearance of his dad and Mr. Mershenson.

John finally said to himself, "Even if other aspects of life do not exist, from now on they will be alive for me." If he had said to anyone that far away there were two persons walking and conversing, he would have been considered a dreamer.

What was true for John couldn't be true for anyone else. What we know for certain, and what we experience, is true for us only, as we cannot experience exactly what someone else feels. John was convinced by this analysis that everyone has the right to believe what they want in their mind. This is also true for our senses and feelings. What one sees, senses and feels is a unique experience that no one else can share. This new reality filled John's mind. Suddenly, a feeling of doubt flickered in John's mind, confusing him. He thought it must be the hot Indian sun that was causing him to have these thoughts. He feared he must have a fever. He felt his forehead to see if he was dreaming and realized that he was sane and sound of mind.

He decided to keep his thoughts to himself and accumulate further experience before he could divulge his thoughts to anyone. He became aware of the danger of not being taken seriously. He remembered his father advising him, "John, there are rules and regulations, there are laws and conventions. They are our guidelines."

John's experiences on this first day did not conform with his father's advice, but he consoled himself that so long as he kept his experiences to himself and in his own mind, he would not breach any convention or law.

John's life became more interesting, as he could play, talk, create and build whatever he wanted in his mind. He discovered that from now on he could be alone but not feel lonely. He no longer had to live solely in society; now he had his private retreat from the tumultuous world. He experienced the same inner sense of peace that he had felt before his mother died. His happiness became his property. No one could penetrate his heart and mind.

This time, John was not prepared to share his experience with his father. He knew that such reasonings were not in his father's line of thought. Why should he take the risk of annoying his father. He knew little of his father's thoughts, just the evening stories.

The sky changed color. The bright gold reflecting from the wheat became almost silver. John quickened his pace to catch up with his father. He was tired but excited and very happy, his face ruddy with color from the sun. He would have preferred to stay in the middle of the field, but it was enough for the first day. He would have time enough to enjoy the landscape with its quaint charm and sense of peace.

He finally reached his father, who was waiting for him. Mr. Mershenson, always well organized, had prepared a pleasant surprise for them. The butler was standing beside the coach, ready to serve lunch. This was turning into a real picnic. A dhurrie was spread out and John sat down right away. This simplicity pleased John, but the butler disturbed the perfect harmony of the landscape. And so did the coach. John wanted to cry aloud, "Don't spoil my view." Mr. Mershenson smiled, thinking he had pleased John with the surprise. John, who did not share this viewpoint, said nothing, so as not to appear impolite. He said to himself, "After all, I shall see what I want to see." The coach and the butler became nonexistent for him.

He enjoyed his lunch, for he was famished. After lunch, the butler served tea. This gave Mr. de Montaigne a good opportunity to return the conversation to business. The fragrant aroma of the tea revived the color in his face. He looked as happy as a child. After all, it was tea that had brought him to India. So far, he had not seen his friend's tea plantation. He did not want to appear too interested in tea. This was a good opportunity. Maybe Mr. Mershenson would talk about his plantation.

Just as he had guessed, Mr. Mershenson said, "This tea is from our plantation."

He was proud of his product. He seemed to have been waiting for lunch to finish. The butler smiled discreetly.

Mr. de Montaigne had waited all morning to hear this remark and, so as not to lose the moment, he immediately asked, "So when are we going to visit your plantation?" Mr. Mershenson did not appear to have heard the question. He stood calmly, apparently deep in thought.

Mr. de Montaigne did not wish to disturb his host and stood up, finished his glass of tea, and was ready to resume his walk. The butler cleared up after them and returned to the coach and coachman. John stood looking quietly, not interfering. He was also ready to continue his walk, for which he had waited politely. Mr. Mershenson led the way, and again John was soon far behind.

He knew that his father's remark had been a pretext to direct the conversation towards business. He did not think the tea had been special. He had also not been entirely concentrating on the tea. Mr. de Montaigne was listening to his friend, but his mind was occupied with tea export. He already calculated the number of tons he could sell. His fortune seemed on hand. He murmured softly, "My friend is for real. I have not wasted my time by coming here." Mr. Mershenson had been putting to him a very important question at the same time, but Mr. de Montaigne, absorbed as he was in his thoughts, had missed it.

Mr. Mershenson asked again, "My friend, so you believe you can sell thousands of tons of tea?"

Mr. de Montnaigne was excited by this question, but he did not want to appear over-eager to do business with his friend. He replied hesitantly and calmly, "The first hundred tons is secured before I came here. Now I shall see what I can do."

Mr. Mershenson was pleased to see his friend anticipating the first hundred tons and answered like a gentleman, "I like this."

Mr. de Montaigne stood taller than before. He felt like a millionaire. He slowed his pace and continued, "I have a friend who will arrive next week from England."

Mr. Mershenson reacted quickly, "The buyer?"

"No," answered Mr. de Montaigne, "He is captain of a merchant ship." For the first time, both gentlemen appeared closer than ever. Mr. Mershenson placed his hand on Mr. de Montaigne's shoulder as a sign of great friendship. This gesture did not go unnoticed by Mr. de Montaigne, who now changed his voice to assert his strength as a businessman. John had missed this business scene. He might have laughed aloud at his father's act.

Mr. Mershenson continued, "You see these fields of wheat? My tea plantation is ten times this size." Mr. de Montaigne was again impressed and as happy as a baby. He suddenly sighed. Mr. Mershenson, thinking his friend was annoyed by his remarks, tactfully changed the subject. Mr. de Montaigne had sighed because he had been thinking of his wife. She did not live to see him become wealthy. She saw only hard work and poverty. A teardrop escaped from the corner of his eye. He hastily wiped it away as if to brush away a dust particle.

John, meanwhile, wandering on his own, had encountered an old gardener, carefully tending flowers. He seemed happy and serious in his work. He diligently bent to pull out every weed. The flowers seemed to respond as if by magic. There were so many shapes, sizes and colors, all unfamiliar to John, facing the sun as if in admiration.

The gardener moved from one to the other as if he knew every one of them. His lips moved as if he were talking to them. The azure sky, the waving fields of wheat, and now these flowers, were in perfect harmony. The wrinkled old gardener seemed to blend right in. All seemed to talk to John and give him a sense of balance and peace. He felt at one with nature. Suddenly, without warning, large drops of rain began to patter down. John had not noticed the dark clouds gather. The rainwater felt warm and was momentary. The sun shone through as if to say, "Don't worry, I am still here." The gardener did not stop in his passionate occupation.

John started to laugh, not knowing why. He felt that rain and sun were both coming from heaven. He then thought of his father. When he was a boy, on their way to school, his father would say to him, "Quick, it may rain." Now, John did not bother to run from this heavenly shower. He stood up straight, his face turned up, feeling the large drops rain down in a deluge. He wanted to be soaked through to the skin. He enjoyed every drop falling on his nose. He no longer feared rain, a wonderful manifestation of the powerful heavens.

The gardener did not notice John's presence. He was absorbed in his flowers like a lover beholding his beloved. John, too, saw the gardener amid the various natural colors and stood in admiration. The old man took care of his flowers conscientiously, undisturbed by the rain.

The downpour lasted a few minutes, then the strong sunrays burst through the clouds. John took hold of himself. His clothes were soon dry, and he continued walking. There was no sign of Mr. Mershenson and his father. Then he saw someone walking towards him from far off. He thought at first that it was his father, concerned about the rain and coming back to see him. Slowly, he realized that the man was dressed differently from his father.

The man walked fast, stirring John's imagination. John stopped for a while to allow the Indian to exchange words with him. John had not spoken a word since morning but was now eager to say a few words. His throat was dry. The gardener had not spoken a word. John assumed that he could at least talk to the flowers.

This thought led to others. He, too, could talk to the sky or to the field. They were certainly not dead objects. They carried a sacred life; maybe they spoke a sacred language that we had yet to discover. He now remembered when his father used to take him to school, which was a few miles from his farm. John would flirt with the trees and with the birds. His father was very patient with him. He never complained, except when he expected it to rain. Many a time, while admiring the bright blue sky, John tripped and fell flat on his face. His father would pick him up without a word, dust him off, and they would continue on their way as if nothing had happened.

Now it was John's turn to be tolerant with his father when he spoke about business with his friend Mershenson. After all, he had worked all his life to fulfill John's needs.

When Mr. de Montaigne was a young married man, he too used to admire the plants on his farm. John now realized that although his father never showed him his sensitive side, he was a good, soft-hearted human being. He never displayed his feelings to anyone. He spoke only about the Bible and his business.

The Indian man was now quite close. John, wondering why he was so attracted by this strange man, did not remember what had happened to him. A sudden frisson passed through his entire body. He felt limp, weak, shaken, and confused.

He thought he must have been hit by a bolt of lightning, but the sky was clear and the sun shone on high. In fact, the sun's rays appeared more intense than ever before. They seemed like a thousand threads of silver from which the earth was suspended.

The old man was now passing him and said a few words which John did not understand. He was not even sure if it was an Indian language. It was decidedly not English. And those miraculous threads now penetrated John's entire being.

The old man laid his hand on John's shoulder as though to calm him. John felt a delicious warmth suffuse his body. He shivered with joy and happiness. While he was still under the spell of this new sensation, the old man was gone.

John was sorry that he could not exchange a few words with the old man. He now realized that the old man wanted to convey a message to him. His words were like sweet music. John felt total peace and silence. He had the distinct impression that he had seen the old man before, but he did not know where.

John continued his walk but had no desire to meet anyone now. He wanted to stay alone to relish the happy sensations as long as he could. The words the old man had said began to come back to him. He memorized them and tried to repeat them. He felt again the sensation of a wonderful stream of electricity on his lips and in his face. He did not understand it, and he did not want to know how it happened.

He knew that the words were for his ears only and that he could repeat them as often as he wanted, but only when he was alone. He felt alive in every atom of his being, something he had never known before. Something new had happened in his life. He knew now what had pulled him all the way from Europe. This was his very own secret which he would have to keep to himself.

These new sensations, new feelings, this whole new world, made him different. In his mind's eye he could see his mother sitting on the step at the farm door, sewing his torn shirt. He recalled the well close to the house and from which his mother used to draw water. All the beautiful days that he had spent on the farm in his childhood came back to life. He tried to push away these visions without knowing why.

The sun's rays started to change color. They became gold mixed with silver. He thought he could remember another world. He pushed away these thoughts, thinking he must be dreaming. He felt the old Indian closer to him than any other person in the whole world.

He hurried along to join his father. Again the butler was there, waiting by the coach to take them back to the house. He realized that since morning he had not seen a single tree. He decided that he did not miss them and could live without them. He wondered if he had really seen any trees before, or if they had been a figment of his imagination.

He reached the coach, where his father and Mr. Mershenson were waiting for him. He recalled the bad memories of his trip on that coach, squeezed between his father and Mr. Mershenson. He considered walking to the estate, so as not to expose his feelings to anyone; he preferred to keep his memories to himself. But he chose to go with his father on the coach. After all, he believed that now, following this new experience, he knew how to avoid suffering. He was confident that nothing could happen to him.

This time John did not feel any discomfort in the coach, and the ride back was quite short. He was plunged in thought with all the feelings he had experienced on his first day in India. No physical trial could diminish the happiness that John now felt. John's conception of time had changed, and he did not find it necessary to converse with anyone.

Upon reaching the house, he went directly to his room and lay down on his bed. He did not feel lonely anymore. He had become his own best companion. He had the impression now that he always had someone to speak to.

Mr. Mershesnon's house was like a palace. The tall columns which held up the ceiling gave an impressive stature to the house. The immense living room was an expression of Mr. Mershenson's wealth. The garden was well tended, but John found that a too regular symmetry in the line of flower beds had disturbed the natural Asian landscape. Personally, he preferred the wheat fields. Of course, he was well advised not to share his opinion with Mr. Mershenson, who was proud of his straight flower lines.

Now John found it easy to play a trick. He would tell Mr. Mershenson what he wanted to hear. He understood that Mr. Mershenson could not accept any criticism, especiallly concerning his garden. He even believed that if Mr. Mershenson knew what John really thought, he would prefer not to hear it. In the evening, John had to dress elegantly, as he knew that Mr. Mershenson liked this kind of life. Clearly, Mr. Mershenson could not imagine even for a moment what was going on in John's mind.

Mr. de Montaigne had prepared John well in playing the games of society. One day he said to John, "If you want to be accepted by your peers, you should first learn to be a good player." Although John knew how to play his part, he was at least sincere at heart and tried not to fall into his own trap.

The second dinner ceremony was more impressive than the first. It was not easy for John to play these parts and be sincere with himself at the same time. He could only relax when he reached his own room, where the four silent walls enabled him to hear his own heart. He could now distinguish a rhythm, which was like a secret language he had learned to translate. The feelings that he had had just a few hours ago became an enigma that he would slowly have to learn to decipher. He had not learned about these feelings and sensations in school. Now, every new experience, with its secret language, would be confirmed in his everyday life.

Suddenly, John's room became brilliantly lit by a flash of lightning, starkly visible through the large window. This was followed by a deafening clap of thunder. Tropical rain came pouring down, and the garden was quickly inundated. The rain seemed inexhaustible.

Water cascaded down from the roof against John's window and splashed on the floor. He got up quickly and closed the windows. The butler hurried in, drenched to the skin. The water streamed down the white walls outside. The fresh smell of rain on dry soil filled every room. Steam rose up from the courtyard, which had been seared by the sun all day long.

Mr. Mershenson went to the library, which was furnished with book-laden shelves along an entire wall. Mr. de Montaigne, smartly dressed, came over to John's room to ask him if he wanted to join him. John, wide awake, accepted gladly. Both gentlemen were now dressed as if for a ceremony. Mr. Mershenson was dressed like a prince, with a white silk scarf. He remarked to his two guests, "Have you ever seen such rain? Without this rain, we would parch here. Now smell the fresh air. In a few moments, the rain will be gone. It is a different world here." John, who had never seen rain like this, agreed with Mr. Mershenson and seemed to be happy. Mr. Mershenson made a small sign with his eyes to the butler.

Three weeks had now passed, with elaborate meals and trips in the coach. Each day was almost like the last. John felt lonely at times, as his father was almost completely occupied with Mr. Mershenson. Mr. de Montaigne's dream was to have a direct link to the tea growers and not to have to go through brokers who could not provide the merchandise most of the time when he had a buyer, and always came up with an excuse for not delivering the promised goods. He had spent his entire life with this problem. Now, a direct deal seemed on hand.

One day he came to John, happy as a boy, and said, "You see, John, all this represents a lot of money. We shall be rich and won't need to travel any longer from city to city and village to village. Just a few shiploads of tea and our problems will be over." He continued, smiling, "You can imagine how lucky we are to have a friend like Mr. Mershenson. I met him when he was in the army. At that time, the British hated the French. He arrived one day, to accompany his General, who had a meeting with our government. One evening he was free from duty and walking about alone, without knowing a word of French. I too was alone, and as I knew English, I volunteered to spend that evening with him. After that, we exchanged friendly letters. He had been born in India and his father was very wealthy. I was young at the time, and all that he said was soon forgotten. But we became good friends. If I had known all this, I would have come much earlier. I would have been rich by now."

Mr. Mershenson did not seem in any hurry to make the deal with his friend. Mr. de Montaigne was patient. This was his last chance.

He was now talking to himself, "It is not easy to become rich. It takes years. We may have to wait patiently for a few weeks, but that is not such a big matter. After all, we are happy here and have everything we need."

For his part, John was happy that the deal was still not made, as he wanted to spend at least a month in India. He had never been as happy as he was now.

SONIA

John had never asked Mr. Mershenson about his daughter. One morning, John was not feeling well. His father advised him to stay home and relax while he and Mr. Mershenson went to Bombay for the day. Around noon, John thought he was dreaming, as he believed he heard footsteps. They were not the slow and heavy footsteps of the butler; these were much lighter. Curious, he opened his door and was surprised to see a pretty young lady walking towards him. He thought at first that she might be a maid. Then he decided that she was too well dressed to be a maid. She passed him without saying a word, but John greeted her, and she returned his greeting with a sweet smile.

John quickly shut the door so as not to appear nosey, but he had wanted to go on gazing at her. He blamed himself for being shy. "I should have started a conversation with her," he muttered to himself. He paced nervously about the room, between the door and the window. When he was quite desperate, someone knocked at his door.

With his heart all aflutter, he hurriedly ran a brush through his hair, took a quick look at himself in the mirror, and then discreetly opened the door.

She was standing there, by the door. John was dumbfounded and nervous. She smiled and, as if to help him over his embarrassment, asked, "Are you John?"

Still stupefied, he put an awkward smile on his face and stammered, "Yes, Miss…?"

"Mershenson," she completed. Then, with an air of confidence and authority, she asked him, "May I come in and have a glimpse of your room to see if you have been treated well?"

John could not have wished for more and answered quickly, "Please do, Miss Mershenson."

"Sonia. It is a very short name," she replied. John was sure he was dreaming. Sonia walked into the room and inspected every corner like an army officer. Then she said, "Do you like this room?"

John, who did not really care for the room, answered, "Oh yes! It's fine, Miss Mershenson."

She corrected him, "Say Sonia."

John obediently repeated, "Yes, Miss Sonia."

"Everyone here calls me 'Miss'. Can't you just call me Sonia?"

John realized he had forgotten to introduce

himself and decided to rectify the situation immediately. "My name is John de Montaigne."

"I know your name, and I know who you are."

John was agreeably confused and could not understand how she knew his name. He then said, "You can call me John."

"No, I would like to call you D.J."

John thought she must be joking. He asked in astonishment, "D.J.?"

"Yes. I like shortened names. I call my father 'Pa', and Miss Gibson I call 'Gibbs'. John could not understand a word of what she was saying.

"Who is Miss Gibson, or Gibbs?" he asked.

At this, Sonia was confused and said with astonishment, "You don't know Miss Gibson?" John was embarrassed at not knowing anything about her, while she seemed to know so much about him. He could not guess who she was and could not see her as Mr. Mershenson's daughter.

He murmured to himself, "She is not a maid, and she cannot be Mr. Mershenson's wife. Maybe she is a sister or a cousin of Mr. Mershenson's." Since he had arrived at this house, he had not seen any women at all. He was, of course, charmed by her presence, but she was still an enigma to him.

Then, suddenly, relief was provided by Sonia

who, upon realizing that John was confused and troubled, said to him softly, "John, sit down for a moment," and she took him by his hand like a child and sat him down on the bed.

John, who was completely enraptured by the touch of her soft hand, sat down on the bed. Without hesitation, Sonia sat down beside him. John's whole being vibrated, as before an exam. She looked into his eyes and said, "John, I can see that you don't know who I am, although I have been thinking about you for years." These words increased John's curiosity; this story was becoming more interesting by the minute. He waited impatiently for her next move.

Sonia continued, "My father's invitation was my idea. Do you know how many times I have dreamed about you? I became obsessed and could hardly study. When you arrived, my father and my teacher did not want me to show up until I had finished my preliminary exams, as they had to be mailed to London. I was furious, but I had to give way to them. Now do you understand?" John was still perplexed and his words were caught in his throat. She continued, "Do you remember one day when I came to Paris with my father? I was ten years old then. You did not even glance at me, but I admired you and looked at you all the time." John could not remember having seen her; he tried hard to think back to find some association with her words but could not find a trace.

She continued, "You have not changed. You are taller and more mature, but your eyes are still the same." John was enchanted with this new adventure; everything seemed to be turning out for him like a delightful romance. Ever since he had left Josephine, he had been eager to meet another young girl. Now everything seemed well arranged, as in a novel. Here he was, alone with a charming young girl.

Her skirt touched his leg once in a while. He wished he had the courage to embrace her, but he was prudent and preferred to wait. He felt already conquered by her charm and her feminine voice.

He was a little embarrassed at the thought of Sonia sitting on his bed. If someone were to enter just now, he would be quite distressed. The thought that his father and Mr. Mershenson might see them both in such a compromising position disturbed him. He wanted to be at his honest best, but at the same time he did not want anyone to disturb these delightful moments that he was enjoying so much. Breaking off from his day dream, he said, "Sonia, can you imagine if your father walked in right now?"

Sonia smiled confidently and said, "My father will not return before evening, and besides, we are doing nothing wrong!"

"But we are together on the same bed!"

Sonia laughed and said, "What would you do if I wanted to kiss you?"

John was disturbed by the thought but was also eager to kiss her, and while he was musing, Sonia, true to her word, hugged him and kissed him. John was thrilled and felt his heart melt. Her warmth was unique. He had never felt like this, even when he was with Josephine. Now a burning fire infused his entire being.

Nothing further happened. Sonia continued, "When I was little, my mother died after a long illness."

John was shocked that someone else had lost her mother and said, "You, too, lost your mother?"

"Yes," she said calmly. "After that my father hired Miss Gibson specially to look after me. She is like my mother, but she is strict with me when it comes to studying. She wants me to be a top student. For what reason, I do not know. They want to shape me, to become a 'good' girl, as they used to say, a girl who dresses well to show that she belongs to high society, a girl who obeys every order and complies with all their traditions and their way of life, a girl who answers as if from a book of rules, a polite girl, a girl with an acquired sense of humor, a girl who laughs when they want me to laugh and is serious when they want me to be serious. There is no room for my imagination, for my spontaneity, for my feelings, for natural enthusiasm. I cannot cry when I want to cry. There is no place for my own choices and likes. I am guided like a robot. No one wants to know about my personality. My personality has to reflect my father's will and his wealth. Do you understand what I am talking about, John?

"Sometimes, I want to be alone, just to remember the song of a bird, the color of a flower, the beautiful colors of roses in bloom, the smell of jasmine, the dark night sky full of stars, or the sunrise that fills our heart with hope and joy and happiness. Simple folk music, colorful design just as Nature intended. Wild trees in their natural shapes. I dream of a garden that grows without the symmetry that my father loves so much. I want to laugh and to cry when I choose. I want to sleep when I am sleepy, to eat when I am hungry. Sometimes, just a piece of bread with something that I like and not to be obliged to eat what our cook has chosen for the day. I have had enough of all those big lunches with the usual ceremony.

"I dream of walking and running when I feel like it, of dressing casually and letting myself be warmed by the sun, of cutting my hair and not being obliged to look like a monkey in a society where everyone tries to impress everyone else, not by their intelligence but by their clothes and wealth.

"I dream of going back to my childhood and hugging my mother and sharing with her my love and my aspirations. I have grown up with Miss Gibbs, whose only duty is to shape me like a living sculpture just for the admiration of others. Who cares about what others think about me! Who cares who I am! I don't want to be like others. I want to be myself, and only myself, with my vast horizon which is not limited to the wealth of my father. I want to write about all my feelings and to cherish you as the person you were for me during all those years, my dream, my only dream. You were my only hope.

"Many a night have I dreamed that you rode on horseback to save me from all my misery and to take me away high in the mountains, close to the sky, where solitude has its own music which thrills my soul and vibrates through my entire being. To see the sun rise and set without saying a word.

"By the way, they use words without value or sense. They don't realize what they are saying. Words have their value and their own strength. Words are the light which illuminates our souls, where every atom of our being becomes transparent and sensitive. Words which make us happy. Words which have profound meaning and which we should treat like gold and not like a fountain in which every drop of water looks alike. Words that tickle my brain and my body. Words which come directly from the spring, clean and pure as crystal, like light and love.

"Words that we use with care and measure as they were the very substance of our lives. Words that identify themselves with all that is beautiful and good. Words which make us feel the sense of good and bad; the sense of light and darkness; words that show us what is right and wrong, justice and injustice, deep and shallow, the north and the south, harmony and discord, warmth and cold, love and hate, the beautiful and the ugly, light and dark. Words that come by themselves to our mind, in solitude, in the rain, in the wind, in the snow and under the blue sky."

Suddenly Sonia awoke as from a dream and said to John, "Oh my God! I think I have talked too much. Do you understand my feelings, do you feel my soul, my pain and my happiness?"

John looked at her silently then said, "As I understand it, you have been confined as though in a cloister?"

"Yes," replied Sonia, "I have led a monastic life."

A few moments earlier, before Sonia made her appearance, John had not been unhappy. Now the presence of this lovely feminine creature had added charm and sense to his life. The thought of the old Indian man who also gave him a sense of his life, confused him. What he had sensed with the old man, and what he now sensed with Sonia, was both agreeable and confusing. He began to have doubts about the real meaning of life.

He thought of his father's story from the Bible, about Adam and Eve and the apple. He tried to reconcile the two pleasant feelings which seemed almost the same. He tried to keep both feelings alive at the same time and realized that a struggle had begun within himself. On the one hand he did not want to lose the sense of purity that he experienced with the presence of the old man. On the other, this new love for Sonia was also strong. John could not decide which path he should follow.

Sonia looked at John, who was lost in thought, and began to prepare a stratagem to conquer John, who appeared to be a virgin and innocent of any feminine contact. Sonia, too, was a virgin and had never had any contact with a man. But she wanted John for herself and herself alone. She was not ready to share his love with anyone else, not even with God. She felt he belonged to her and to her alone. John had been a part of her for so many years. She was afraid someone would tear away the Prince Charming of whom she had dreamed on so many nights since her childhood.

The idea that John's silence possibly meant there was another woman in his life disturbed her and made her furious. She did not show this feeling to John, who sat helplessly like a child before his teacher. The presence of John next to her awakened her whole being like a flower under the sun. Suddenly, the thought that her father was due to return from Bombay made her nervous. Then she calmed down, knowing her father loved to show others what a good guide he was.

A total silence now filled the room. It

was broken by the sound of the butler coming to announce that it was time for lunch. John instinctively jumped up from the bed and sat down quickly on a chair, like a thief. This feeling of guilt disturbed him. Sonia was cool; she did not move from the bed. The butler did not impress her anymore. She had no fear. John's face changed color several times. When the butler knocked on the door, John's heart palpitated. Sonia, who was familiar with the rules of the society in which she lived, called out, "We have just eaten some fruit. Please have some soup ready for dinner. I want to wait till father returns. Thank you!"

John admired Sonia's composure and authority. He said to himself, "She plays the part perfectly."

Sonia smiled confidently and said to him, "Don't you like your bed?"

John, embarrassed, replied immediately, "Oh no! I like the bed!"

Then she asked, "Are you afraid of the butler?" John did not have an answer to this question; this kind of life was completely new to him. Sonia again came towards him, took his hand, and led him to the bed, where they sat down. Without knowing how, John took advantage of the moment and, without a word, hugged her and kissed her face. He felt as happy as a child, so good, so pleased. He thought he was dreaming, but this was no dream. This was the reality that he had waited so long for. Now everything seemed to fulfil all his hopes and dreams. The old Indian man, whom he had encountered during his first day while he was walking through the field of wheat, now became more comprehensible and more of a reality. He felt he had to share his sensations and happiness with Sonia. Then he decided to stay silent and to enjoy the pleasure of the current of love which was passing through his body and his soul.

Every moment's silence became more precious than the greatest wealth on earth. He looked at Sonia's eyes. They were so deep, like water at the bottom of a well. Her face now seemed younger than at the first moment he had seen her. Her skin was softer than that of a baby. They looked at each other with happiness and love; something very powerful seemed to capture them both and to embrace them with a sweet soft ray of love. Neither had ever experienced such a feeling. They stayed silent for a long time, hoping no one would disturb this beautiful feeling which came to them like grace.

The room was filled with a kind of vibration.

Both John and Sonia experienced a feeling of serenity, security, and peace. This was a unique moment, a moment of kindness and love, which had nothing to do with physical love. A love of just being together. To be next to each other. The beauty of life was unveiled to both of them like magic. They lived in another world, a dream-world that mankind had never known before, except maybe in a few mystical books or in the Bible. John remembered his father talking about the love of Jesus and his apostles.

And here he was in the country of Mantras and high castes, the country with the high mountains whose summits no man had ever reached, so different from the kind of life that he knew from his father's stories. One day his father told him about a holiday resort where the well-heeled spent their holidays in luxury; where the ladies and the men were all large and obese.

In the same resort there were thin women masseuses who massaged the fat ladies to dissolve the fat that they accumulated with the rich food. They did nothing else but sit and eat and breathe the fresh air. Their conversation was uninteresting. All they talked about was business and money, their big houses, the number of maids they had, and the gold jewelry that covered their arms and necks.

The men spent their days analyzing every woman and trying to imagine her body under her voluminous clothes. The men were no thinner. Their stomachs hung like balloons over their bodies. During the massage hour they were served all kinds of food, just so that they would never be hungry. What irony! What a ridiculous life they had! Mr. Mershenson was the kind of man that John's father had described.

Now, food became trivial to the existence of John and Sonia. They appreciated every minute of life. They contemplated the trees, the flowers; the entire landscape had its charm. The air they breathed was the essence of their daily life. They had spent over five hours together in the same room, without feeling the need to eat anything. Nothing was more important to them than to maintain this lovely atmosphere, which nourished them with the taste of real life and brought every atom of their bodies to life as they had never felt before.

It was almost six o'clock, and the sun started to fade and make place for the moon and the stars. The sky had a reddish tinge, which indicated the prelude of another nice day and alerted them to be prepared to face the world of comedy and nonsense again, the world of food and ceremony. Any minute now their fathers would return from Bombay. It was hard for them to leave this wonderful world and return to the world of irony and comedy. They had no choice. They both now knew that they had to keep this wonderful feeling alive for themselves until the next occasion…

Meanwhile, the telephone rang. It was Mr. Mershenson calling from Bombay. He instructed the butler to tell Sonia and John not to wait up for them, as they would be staying overnight in Bombay.

When the butler again knocked on John's door, John was completely unnerved. This time he was sure that his father and Mr. Mershenson had arrived earlier than expected. He saw the end of his romance with Sonia. The butler's voice interrupted his thoughts. "Miss Sonia, your father just called and asked you to excuse him for tonight, as he has to stay overnight in Bombay. He will be arriving tomorrow."

Sonia nonchalantly answered, "Thank you!" Now, both young people were completely free from having to go to dinner and from interruption by their fathers. They now had all night to themselves. Sonia again smiled as if to say, "Don't worry, everything is working out according to my dreams and wishes."

In the morning, John awoke and was surprised to find himself alone in bed. He thought that he had had a wonderful dream. He wondered if Sonia's presence had been real or just an Asian mirage. He tried to go back to sleep in order to revive the dream, when Sonia knocked on his door. John was completely confused. He jumped up from his bed. He could not clearly remember what had happened the day before. He was still on the borderline between sleep and wakefulness. He was sure Sonia had been sitting on his bed. He hoped their relationship had stopped while it was yet platonic, as he did not want to lose her.

John was convinced this time that he loved her with all his heart. Sonia was already dressed in riding breeches. She was smiling and, as usual, sure of herself. She asked him if he would like to accompany her on a horse ride. John, who had never ridden a horse in his life, smiled and answered, "I would love to, if you could teach me how."

Sonia confidently replied, "Of course I will teach you." John was embarrassed, as he was not yet dressed. He asked her if she would like to wait for him, as he wanted to take a shower. Sonia calmly indicated that she would. John waited for her to leave, but she walked right into his room and began to make his bed, while he went to take a shower.

Coming out of the shower, John realized that he had not brought a change of clothes with him. He put on his pants from the day before and came out. As he opened the door, Sonia was standing there, waiting for him. She grabbed his hand and kissed him. John, who was still wet, his hair disheveled, was embarrassed. She helped him button his shirt and continued to watch him as he pulled on his socks and shoes. Sonia knew that her father would be back in the afternoon and did not want to miss the opportunity of having John all to herself in the fields in which she had dreamed of being for a long time.

She had already ordered the stable hand to saddle two horses. John was famished, as he had not eaten the night before. Breakfast was waiting for them outside on a well-laid table. John felt that he was being treated with the sort of attention that he had never received before. Everything was so well planned. Sonia had rehearsed just such an occasion in her mind countless times. She knew every step and every movement. Many a time she had spent in the field dreaming about John. Now everything was turning into reality. She had only to take the reins in her hand. No one would change her mind about John, and no one would dare take John from her. John belonged to her and to her only.

Now it was a question of proving her love to John. She had already realized that John was very receptive to her touch and her presence. Her father had a fortune which would all go to her and John, sufficient means for their entire life. From now on she saw her happiness secured. Even her father, with his strong personality and authority, would not be able to resist her will. The servants and the butler respected Sonia even more than they did her father. Since her youth, she had always known how to impose her personality.

One day her father had thrown a party. Every notable personality was present. Her father kept telling her about the Governor and his influence. She immediately decided not to be over-impressed. When the Governor arrived, impeccably dressed, Sonia was there to receive him. When he tried to impress her with his attire and rank, Sonia whispered something in his ear. The Governor was momentarily taken aback, his face fell, and he appeared very subdued for the rest of the evening.

After the party, Sonia laughed alone in her room, relishing her little trick. She recounted the story one day to her father, when he asked her why the Governor had been so quiet. She told her father what she had whispered in his ear. She had told the Governor that his shirt had a dirt mark on it, and if he kept his arm against his side, it would not be visible. Since then, Sonia had had a good relationship with the Governor.

The two horses were saddled and ready for Sonia and John. The butler asked her if she needed an escort to accompany them. Her answer was a firm "No."

John was completely taken by Sonia's attitude. He said to her, "Sonia, we won't be here when our fathers arrive."

Sonia, smiling, replied, "Don't worry, they won't miss us, and we shall surprise them. After all, they enjoyed their day in Bombay without us. Now it's our turn to enjoy our day without them."

John did not want to argue with Sonia, as he was only too happy to be able to spend a day in the fields with her. His question had only been a matter of form. The butler, knowing Sonia well, had taken care to prepare food and drink for the day. But he did not avoid showing his displeasure.

Sonia noticed it and in turn grimaced back.

John hid his happiness. He loved the vista spread out before them, and the company of the charming Sonia made him even happier. He too had dreamed about such an adventure when he was young, but he never knew who his partner would be. Sonia seemed to fit the role naturally. The last trip had been a pleasant one, although he had been alone. Now he would discover more beauty. This time Sonia would surely reveal many beautiful places to him. She must know some special place that even her father had not discovered. Her romanticism was different from her father's.

Sonia was an excellent and very experienced rider. Nature would be the witness of her love for John. It would certainly show its beauty to John in another light. Although she knew that John was conquered by her charm, she wanted to reaffirm her conquest. She would now have to teach John how to ride. This would take her an hour or two. Then she would turn her dreams into reality.

Both John and Sonia rode very slowly. John had a gentle horse that seemed to understand that he had never ridden before. Once in a while, John lost his balance and his seat, but each time he succeeded in falling without hurting himself. Soon, John and Sonia were far from the estate. They were completely alone. John was not too confident about riding. Once in a while he led the horse by the reins. The horse was pleased. Sonia had to be tolerant, and in order not to embarrass John, she walked too. They had to reach a certain place, from where she could show John a unique spot. After walking a while she said to John, "Now I shall teach you how to gallop."

John was afraid but did not want to show weakness. Sonia was ahead of him, and every now and then she turned her head to see if he was following her. Everything seemed perfect. Then the place she was looking for came in sight. Sonia felt excited and nervous for the first time. She knew that from this moment on, John would be hers forever. She was so consumed by her thoughts that she had forgotten to keep her eye on John. Suddenly she remembered him. She turned her head but could see no trace of him.

Her first thought was that he knew how to ride and was playing games with her, hiding with his horse. She rode back to look for him but couldn't see him anywhere. Then she began to shout, "John, you win! Where are you?" John did not respond. Sonia was now agitated. She began to search frantically, when suddenly she saw the horse standing alone at a distance. She thought maybe John had chosen a nice place for himself. Then she decided John was too polite and serious to do something like that. She began to feel her dream was in danger of never being fulfilled.

When she reached the horse, she saw John lying on the ground unconscious. She shook him, but he did not respond. She realized that he had fallen from his horse and was seriously hurt. His face was not its usual color. She began to cry helplessly. Then she decided to ride back quickly to the estate and get a doctor. She rode off, leaving John lying unconscious on the ground.

Meanwhile, Mr. Mershenson and Mr. de Montaigne had returned to the estate. When the butler told them that Sonia and John had ridden out on the estate, Mr. de Montaigne was deeply concerned, as he knew John did not know how to ride. They decided to go look for the young people. They got into the coach and started out in the direction indicated by the butler.

After a while, Mr. Mershenson discovered the horse grazing by itself. He pointed it out to Mr. de Montaigne, "You see the horse? They must be here." When they reached the horse, they discovered John unconscious on the ground. Mr. Mershenson shouted loudly, "Sonia!" No answer, and no trace of the second horse. Both gentlemen were now alarmed. They must surely have been attacked by the lawless bandits that roamed these lands, and Sonia must have been kidnapped.

Sonia took shortcuts through the fields on her way back to the estate. Many jumbled thoughts passed through her mind. She was not sure if John was alive. She blamed herself for making him ride a horse. She was in dire distress. All her dreams and plans seemed to have reached a sudden end. Her eyes filled with tears, and her heart felt laden with guilt. Suddenly a spark of hope was kindled in her heart, "My God, if John suddenly awakes and does not find me next to him, he may think I have abandoned him." She had half a mind to turn back, even though the estate was within sight. She saw his handsome face in her mind's eye, and the wavy hair that she loved so much. She longed to hold him, and she blamed herself for not having left a note by his side.

While Mr Mershenson was full of concern about his daughter's disappearance, Mr. de Montaigne, sitting beside his unconscious son, was anxiously checking his pulse. His face lit up when he felt the faint beating of John's heart. Now it was only a question of time. John would awake momentarily. He felt relieved that at least John was alive, thank Heavens.

Reassured about his son, he joined Mr. Mershenson who was standing at a distance, filled with despair, and tried to calm him down. Both gentlemen tried to think what could have happened, like a pair of detectives. Mr. de Montaigne's optimism gave Mr. Mershenson reason for hope. Soon they saw a coach approaching at a distance. They ran to the middle of the road and waved to the coachman to stop. He was coming towards them at considerable speed. They could not figure out who the person in the coach might be, since the entire area was private, including the roadway. Then they heard Sonia's voice screaming, "Daddy! Daddy! Is John alive?" The coach came to a halt, and a tearful Sonia, accompanied by the family doctor, stepped down.

Mr. de Montaigne, who did not know the doctor, was reassured when Mr. Mershenson told him that this was his friend, Dr. Desquin. He had recovered from the shock he had had, and his anxiety began to fade. Relief was near; John would regain consciousness, and this unfortunate incident would be quickly forgotten. At the same time he thought that, because of this sad incident, Mr. Mershenson would feel himself tied more closely to him, and he hoped that this would help him pull off the big tea deal. All these mixed feelings upset Mr. de Montaigne, especially as he thought about the tea business while his son still lay on the hard, stony ground.

The doctor checked John and was quick with his diagnosis. "The young man is alright. He was just knocked unconscious. Let us take him to the house; after a few hours' sleep he will awake normally." These words warmed the heart of Mr. de Montaigne, and especially Sonia.

Sonia regained her confidence and began to think how she would take care of John. She said to her father, "Daddy, I will take care of John. I want to be with him when he comes to."

Mr. Mershenson, who saw the tears in Sonia's eyes, answered with more warmth than usual, "Yes, darling, you will take care of him. Now wipe away those tears. Everything will be alright." The three gentlemen carefully lifted John into the doctor's coach. Sonia took John's head in her lap. She held him with tender care, and all through the trip she did not stop admiring

John's face and gently stroking his hair.

She was happy, but distressed. She prayed for him. This was the first time that Sonia had ever prayed for anyone. She loved him so much that from now on nothing would deter her from marrying him. With this unfortunate accident, her father would probably be more tolerant and receptive to her feelings.

It was the first time in years that Mr. Mershenson had seen his daughter in tears, and it broke his heart. All his life his only dream had been to see Sonia happy.

When they reached the house, John was carefully carried in by four servants who laid him on Sonia's bed, by her express orders. Her room was spacious, and her bed was as grand as that of a princess.

The next day, John was breathing normally, but he had not regained consciousness as quickly as the doctor had predicted. Sonia was alarmed and confused at the state of her beloved John. The doctor came early, expecting to find John awake and in good shape, and was disturbed at his condition. After briefly examining him once again, he decided to take him to the hospital in Bombay. Sonia again joined him, and behind the doctor's coach the Mershenson coach followed with Mr. de Montaigne, who was in dire distress for his son and his business. He saw his long trip ending miserably. He saw himself alone once again, and at his age this made him sad and disoriented.

The trip was long. Sonia's tears dropped incessantly onto John's face. The doctor was also upset and would have liked to comfort Sonia, but he knew that Sonia mistrusted him, as his prognosis had been wrong the day before.

THE HOSPITAL

When they reached the hospital, it was already late in the afternoon. The hospital's chief doctor took John in charge and suggested that Sonia stay in the waiting room with her doctor until he had thoroughly examined John. Mr. Mershenson and his friend arrived a half hour later, completely exhausted from the trip and from emotion.

Mr. de Montaigne hurried in first, out of breath. His first question to the doctor was, "How is John?"

Dr. Desquin, though uncertain, said calmly, "The chief doctor has personally taken him in charge." This reply did not mean anything to the two parents who were eager to receive comforting news. All four sat looking at each other, without exchanging a word, each lost in dramatic thoughts unknown to the other.

Sonia spontaneously stood up, sat down next to Mr. de Montaigne and took his hand in her own. She felt closer to him than to her own father. This little scene did not pass unnoticed by Mr. Mershenson, who, for the first time, felt abandoned by his daughter, and alone. All his wealth had no meaning anymore. He had spent his entire life making a fortune, just to provide amply for his daughter and make her happy. Then, without a word, he joined Mr. de Montaigne, taking his other hand firmly in his own, as if to say, "We are together in this; we are a family."

This incident made Mr. de Montaigne even more morose. He felt as if John was dying and the hands of Sonia and Mr. Mershenson were there to console him in his distress. His heart felt heavy. He did not want to survive John. The tragedy of his wife's death was enough. He could not survive another tragedy.

The doctor sat alone at the other end of the room, feeling guilty for not having diagnosed John's case accurately. Once in a while, through an open door, one could see nurses running back and forth. The atmosphere was tense. Outside, the sun had set, and nightfall was gradually settling in. The silence burdened the already heavy atmosphere.

Miss Gibson, who had been absent for a few days, returned a few hours after John's coach had left for Bombay. When she heard the news, she was deeply disturbed and blamed herself for having taken a few days off. Her main concern was not for John's well-being, as she had never had the opportunity to meet him. During John's arrival, Miss Gibson had been busy with Sonia's studies. Her main objective was to prepare Sonia for her exams. She was now afraid that Sonia would suffer a shock and be unable to concentrate during the crucial days before the final exams.

Dr. Walls, chief doctor at the hospital, came to the waiting room, his face haggard with exhaustion. He was very serious. He was still in his white coat. All looked at him expectantly. No one dared ask the inevitable question. Finally, Mr. Mershenson couldn't stand the silence any longer and blurted out, "Doctor, is he alive?"

Dr. Walls briefly answered, "Yes". He then called Dr. Desquin to join him. A cold sweat passed over Sonia, who had been rooted to the waiting room.

Mr. de Montaigne collapsed into his chair with a "Thank God!"

Dr. Desquin fell in step beside Dr. Walls, who was taking off his white coat. Both doctors slowed down and looked at each other gravely. Dr. Desquin said, "Well, Dr. Walls, is it serious?"

"A leg fracture, a hip fracture, a broken rib and, most disturbing, a cranial injury."

Dr. Desquin interrupted with, "Yes, that's what makes me nervous. Mr. Mershenson happens to be my best patient."

"I know."

"And his guest is so young."

Dr. Walls did not want to continue in this vein. He excused himself with, "I must hurry along. I have another serious case waiting."

Dr. Desquin, a general practitioner, felt his limitations in front of such a skilled physician and immediately answered, "Of course, Dr. Walls." Dr. Walls rushed off, leaving Dr. Desquin standing in the empty corridor, wondering how he was going to break the news to his most valued patient. He then took a hold of himself and ventured into the waiting room. Once there, he said, in a calm and professional manner, "Well, now we can all go home and have a drink. John is safe and will be out of the hospital soon."

Mr. Mershenson, who had been most concerned and embarrassed for his friend, requested that Dr. Desquin stay in the hospital and keep a close watch on John. Dr. Desquin, whose feelings of guilt had not yet deserted him, complied without hesitation. Mr. de Montaigne thanked Dr. Desquin and went with Sonia and her father towards the coach. Sonia wanted to stay close to John, but her father gently led her away with, "Sonia, wouldn't you love to have a drink with Mr. de Montaigne?"

"Oh yes!" answered Sonia, knowing well that Mr. de Montaigne should not be left alone at such a time.

Dr. Desquin remained alone in the waiting room. He was not yet at ease with himself, first for not having been honest with his best patient, and then he was concerned about John's condition after hearing Dr. Walls's report. He knew the rib fracture might take a long time to heal, but the injury to the hip joint might very well handicap him for the rest of his life. The tibial fracture did not overly worry him. His major cause for concern was the cranial injury. He knew that John could eventually suffer cranial trauma, which, even if he came through well, might result in amnesia.

He knew that sooner or later he would have to tell at least Mr. Mershenson how matters stood. He tried to calm himself by reasoning that this was not the best time, especially with Sonia and Mr. de Montaigne around. He knew the consequences of giving false hope, but he was so disturbed that he preferred to wait till the next day... maybe all his worry would prove unnecessary.

He decided to wait as long as necessary to meet Dr. Walls again and to discuss the matter with him, without pressure. If he was lucky, he might even convince Dr. Walls to dine with him.

While Dr. Desquin was thus lost in his thoughts, he saw Dr. Walls's two assistants emerge from the operating theatre. He thought of intercepting them, then held back, thinking any discussion with Dr. Walls's assistants might jeopardize his meeting with Dr. Walls, for whom he had a great deal of respect.

John was then wheeled out on a stretcher, accompanied by two nurses, their faces grave and concerned. Presently Dr. Walls hurried out, this time dressed and looking as if was heading for home. Dr. Desquin intercepted him and invited him to dinner. Dr. Walls politely refused, saying he was exhausted and had to perform an operation early the next day.

Dr. Desquin realized that he would not be able to persuade Dr. Walls and asked him if it might be a good idea for him to spend the night next to John. At this, Dr. Walls shrugged his shoulders, indicating, "If you wish." Dr. Desquin noticed that Dr. Walls seemed to be preoccupied with something and decided to press him.

He repeated, "As I understand it, you agree to my spending the night at John's bedside?"

"Yes," said Dr. Walls, and continued, "Soon, all the doctors will have to spend the night here."

"Is John's condition that serious?" demanded Dr. Desquin, John alone on his mind.

"I am not thinking of John."

"Well?"

"I am thinking of the dreaded disease," said Dr. Walls, lighting a cigarette.

"What disease?"

"Cholera!"

"John has cholera?" was Dr. Desquin's quizzical remark.

"No, no! I had reports today of two people who have died of cholera," Dr. Walls explained, now seemingly more willing to discuss the matter with Dr. Desquin.

"My God! Do we have an epidemic?"

"Maybe." This from a nonchalant Dr. Walls.

"What do you mean by 'maybe'? Either you know that we do, or you don't!"

"We shall just have to wait and see," said Dr. Walls.

"Oh, my God! I'd rather not think about this," said an agitated Dr. Desquin, still thinking only about John.

Dr. Walls instructed Dr. Desquin to take all the necessary measures and be on standby in the event that an epidemic was confirmed. Then, in a serious, clinical tone, he said, "At least we professionals will be ready to do our duty."

"What duty?" inquired Dr. Desquin, a hint of irony in his tone. "To confirm the dead? We have no professional manpower and no drugs."

Dr. Walls looked earnestly at Dr. Desquin and replied, "I have been trying to get this hospital into functional shape for years. London's response has typically been: 'Do what you can with what you have. We have no budget, or the budget for this year is already depleted.' That is the sort of answer I have come to expect from the authorities each time we put our requests in writing. You understand, don't you?"

Dr. Desquin felt pleased at the appeal in Dr. Walls's voice. Dr. Walls went on, "They think that we doctors can solve these problems with answers like that. They want their colonies, but they couldn't care less for the well-being of the locals. Had we asked for ammunition or soldiers, it would be here before you could bat an eyelid. For that they always have a contingency budget."

Dr. Desquin, who had never dealt with the

administration, responded naively, "Suppose we telegraphed His Majesty, King Edward?" and thinking he had found an ingenious solution, he looked expectantly at Dr. Walls.

His face fell at Dr. Walls's disparaging response. "My dear man, you are naive. Do you think the telegram would ever reach the King? His Majesty will receive a nice little report of what the administration wants to show him. Do you know what these reports look like?"

"No," answered Dr. Desquin, by now feeling disappointed and ill-informed.

"Let me tell you. The reports will always look good, so that His Majesty can enjoy his breakfast."

Dr. Desquin, whose first concern was his patients, tried to think of an explanation for such a remark. He was disturbed by this report of the administration's attitude. He had always been proud to be the product of a civilized nation like Great Britain. He exclaimed, "Do you mean to tell me that our government does not care about the local population? What are we here for, then?"

Dr. Walls said sardonically, "My dear sir, what on earth gave you the idea that we are here to help the Indians? Let's be honest. We are here to protect our economic interests. Of course, we give enough to the populace to get their cooperation."

Dr. Desquin, who had been so preoccupied earlier with John's well-being, was now so deep in political discussion with Dr. Walls that he had quite forgotten John for the moment. He replied, "This is awful. What are you telling me about our government?"

"Oh, don't worry. You are half French and, if I am not mistaken, you were born in the French colony of Pondicherry."

"What has my birthplace got to do with all this? I am British!" declared Dr. Desquin roundly.

Dr. Walls, feeling that he had overstepped the mark, continued on a more conciliatory note, "I just want to tell you that the French government is no different from our government. But don't worry, my friend…"

Dr. Desquin, on being addressed as "my friend" by no less a personage than the renowned Dr. Walls, was pleased in spite of himself.

"Don't worry. Sooner or later our roles will change. When these natives get educated and conscious of their power, they will be able to take their lives and their economy into their own hands. They will dictate to us the way they choose to live and, if they are nice, they may pardon our conduct and our arrogance."

Dr. Desquin, who was quite flustered at the turn the conversation was taking, asked Dr. Walls, "And do you, Dr. Walls, condone what we, as British subjects, are doing?"

"My dear Desquin, I am here to fulfill my duty as a physician, and I try my darndest without any discrimination. Fortunately or otherwise, I am not a politician and not a military man. What we can do is involve the army in this epidemic."

"How?" inquired Dr. Desquin, to whom Dr. Walls represented the light at the end of the tunnel.

"I need your help and your trust."

"You have my trust." This from a fervent Dr. Desquin.

"Just wait and see how quickly we get a reaction from London."

"I shall do whatever is necessary. You can count on me," said Dr. Desquin devotedly. Dr. Walls felt reassured of Dr. Desquin's support.

"We shall have to involve the Governor, too," said Dr. Walls, confident now. Then he added, with enthusiasm, "That is very simple. We can demand to check the soldiers, so that the epidemic does not spread within our army."

"That is a great solution, but the army doctors may be opposed to such an inspection."

"Don't worry. We doctors speak a common language; and after all, we are trying to help. Of course, we shall be very professional. The army doctors will be happy not to have to carry the burden. We shall select a few soldiers whom we shall diagnose as suspected cholera cases."

"You are a genius," interrupted Dr. Desquin, pink with suppressed excitement at Dr. Walls's calculated malice. He continued, "We shall then admit these soldiers into our hospital for observation. You know what I mean. The rest you can imagine."

Dr. Desquin, eager to solve the problem, said, "When do we begin? Now?"

"No. Tomorrow," answered Dr. Walls, quite devoid of any excitement.

Dr. Desquin, who had never had occasion to be so close to Dr. Walls, did not want to let the opportunity slip by and asked Dr. Walls again, "Where are you going to dine tonight, Dr. Walls?"

"Oh, I shall snatch a bite to eat somewhere."

"Are you alone?"

"Yes."

"Why don't you come over with me? My

wife is French, and I am sure we shall enjoy a good French meal together. This morning, before we left home to come to Bombay, she told me that she would prepare a surprise meal for me, something that I have never had since our wedding. I am sure it will be delicious. I dropped her off at our house in town."

Dr. Walls, who already felt involved with Dr. Desquin and did not want to compromise his collaboration, graciously accepted this time and added, "But we shall have to return to the hospital after dinner, as John will have recovered from the anesthesia."

Mrs. Desquin, who came from good French stock, had spent the entire day in the kitchen preparing an English dinner for the first time, to surprise her husband. After all, she thought, it will be amusing for a French woman to cook an English meal, and so that everything would be just so, she had invited her young English friend to help.

Dr. Walls was charmed by Mrs. Desquin and her friend. He was still a bachelor, and the presence of a young single lady was welcome, although he had looked forward to a good French meal after his exhausting day. Eyeing the tastefully served dishes, he said, "I see you must have had an interesting day, cooking an English meal. I am certain it will taste better than any English meal prepared by any English woman," he remarked galantly, unaware that Mrs. Desquin's friend was English.

Mrs. Desquin, sensitive to her friend's feelings, said tactfully, "Doctor, if the meal tastes good, all credit should go to Josephine; I have merely selected the French wine."

"Marvellous," said Dr. Walls, his mind still preoccupied with the hospital patients and the fear of impending cholera, which was weighing down on him. The ladies smiled at each other at Dr. Walls's next remark, "Interesting evening! English food with French wine!"

A short monsoon rain suddenly splattered down, leaving behind the refreshing smell of jasmine and moist earth which drifted into the dining room through the wide-open windows. Mrs. Desquin, though of French ancestry, was born in India and had spent many years studying in Paris. She spoke English beautifully, with a slight French accent, which added to her charm. The Desquin children were away, temporarily schooling in France, and Mrs. Desquin could not bear the loneliness of their big, beautiful home. She was very happy to be entertaining the renowned Dr. Walls.

She was well acquainted with the wives of all the doctors, who spoke about nothing except their husbands' patients and their husbands' practices. As they were finishing the savory hors d'oeuvres, the telephone rang. It was Dr. Gering from the laboratory, desperately trying to trace Dr. Walls. Dr. Desquin took the call.

"Dr. Desquin, I have been trying for over an hour to reach Dr. Walls. Someone in the hospital saw you leaving with him. Would you happen to know where I could find him?"

Dr. Desquin, who had a good idea of what the message would be, answered quickly, "He is here with me, but if the message is not urgent, I would rather he finished his dinner."

Dr. Gering apologized and left a message, "Will you please tell him that it has been confirmed."

Dr. Desquin returned to the table with a set smile, as he had no desire to ruin the appetite of his special guest who seemed to be enjoying himself a great deal. His professional conscience would not let him rest, however. The main course over, Mrs. Desquin repaired to the kitchen to give instructions for dessert to be served. Dr. Desquin excused himself and followed her, to tell her not to insist on dessert. Mrs. Desquin had a good mind to insist but knew her husband well enough and decided to defer to his judgement. Dr. Desquin bent over Dr. Walls and informed him of Dr. Gering's phone call.

Dr. Walls, with great tact and sensitivity to the ladies' feelings, stood up and said, "My dear ladies, I am afraid I cannot stay for dessert."

Josephine, who had noticed none of the undercurrents and was hoping to enjoy Dr. Walls's company over champagne, said petulantly, "But Dr. Walls, you will miss the best part of the evening!"

Dr. Walls answered, "And no one sorrier than I to miss such charming company. However, duty calls! I have a patient who will be waking up from anesthesia, and I must be at hand to see his reaction." This was, of course, not the true reason, but he did not want to mention the word cholera. This would create a panic among the ladies, who he was sure would spread the word like wildfire.

Mrs. Desquin, to save the situation, said in a lighter vein to Josephine, "Josephine, dear, did I not tell you only today not to marry a doctor if you do not wish to be alone? They have a sacred duty to fulfill," and turning to Dr. Walls she continued, "Dr. Walls, I am sorry not to have you with us for dessert, but being a doctor's wife, I understand."

Dr. Walls excused himself profusely and was walked to the door by Dr. Desquin, who offered to drive him to the hospital. They continued their conversation in an undertone. "My dear friend, this is a catastrophe! Please drop me off at the laboratory and I shall join you later in the hospital. Please inform my assistant discreetly, and tell your wife that you will be absent for the night."

Both doctors proceeded to the hospital, leaving the two ladies to entertain themselves as best they could. Mrs. Desquin, who did not want to ruin the evening, said to Josephine, "Let's have some champagne. I am determined to have a good time despite their absence."

Josephine, with no inkling of the connection between Dr. Desquin, John, and Mr. Mershenson, and drawn out by the good wine and cozy atmosphere, recounted her adventure with John on board ship.

Mrs. Desquin's first question was, "Is he a doctor?"

"No," answered Josephine.

"Thank God!" exclaimed Mrs. Desquin,

"At least you will enjoy your evenings without interruption. You see what it is like being married to a doctor?"

Josephine, who was very young and had very few friends, smiled and said, "I wonder where I could find him."

"Don't worry," answered Mrs. Desquin, "my husband knows everyone within the European community, and I could easily find out. Let us first enjoy the evening, and you can sleep over tonight, as my husband told me that he will have to spend the night at the hospital, assisting Dr. Walls."

Mrs. Desquin knew that her husband was taking care of a young guest of the Mershenson family, but she did not know that this was the same young man that Josephine was talking about. Mrs. Desquin realized through Josephine's conversation that she was in love with this young Frenchman. She felt a little envious of Josephine's love, as she too had wished to marry a Frenchman, and especially not a doctor. She said to Josephine, "I am glad my children are in Paris. At least I know they are happy there. If they were here, they would never see their father anyway. But in my time it was an honor to have a doctor for a husband." She remembered her honeymoon night, when her husband had had to leave her alone. At the time she had been furious, but now she was glad to have so much time for herself. She had become accustomed to this kind of life and was always entertaining guests, mostly the wives of other doctors.

Josephine listened to Mrs. Desquin with great curiosity and interest. It was a novelty for her to be talking with a married woman. She did not know too much about women or marriage. She had spent most of her time with her old father. She accepted Mrs. Desquin's offer to stay overnight, after having called her father, who readily agreed, knowing his daughter was in good hands.

Dr. Walls went straight to the laboratory. Dr. Gering was there, having waited long for a call from him. Dr. Walls adjusted an experienced eye over the eyepiece of the compound microscope and fidgeted briefly to bring the glass slide into precise focus on the now stained and immobile bacteria.

"Vibrio comma! Just as I thought."

"Well, it is thanks to Dr. Koch that I was able to identify the bacteria," said Dr. Gering.

"Yes, you Germans are the most brilliant

scientists on earth. What would we do without you?" Then, casting a piercing glance at him, Dr. Walls continued, "Not a word about this to anyone. We do not want the entire population on our backs."

Dr. Gering, pleased at Dr. Walls's praise, replied, "I shan't say a word to anyone, though we must notify the authorities."

"Leave that to me. Just follow my instructions." Dr. Gering had much respect for Dr. Walls, especially since he was the one who had recommended him for the laboratory chief's post. He turned off the lights, and both gentlemen stepped out.

Dr. Walls joined Dr. Desquin, who was in despair at finding John still unconscious. On seeing Dr. Walls, he shook his head in despair. Dr. Walls motioned to him to join him. Without losing a minute he said, "Take me to the Governor's mansion, Desquin."

When they were halfway there, Dr. Desquin asked, "You want to see the Governor at this late hour?"

"Yes. This is the best time. I know that he is giving a reception for a royal personage from England. He must be awake."

They reached the Governor's palace and,

true to Dr. Walls's prediction, the palace was fully lit and buzzing with activity. Dr. Walls had a long discussion with the uniformed sepoy, who did not know him, and was finally ushered into the Governor's presence. Opulently dressed guests mingled with the dignitaries. The nonchalant Dr. Walls in his grey suit succeeded in raising a few eyebrows.

The Governor, who was well acquainted with Dr. Walls and his reputation, greeted him warmly. Dr. Walls requested a private audience. The Governor excused himself from his guests and they stepped into a small, private anteroom. The Governor knew that Dr. Walls would never encroach at this late hour without good reason and came directly to the point.

"Is there a problem, Doctor?"

"We certainly have a problem," was the cool reply.

"Personal?"

"No, no!" The Governor became more attentive at Dr. Walls's grave tone. "It's very serious, sir. I need your written permission to inspect Army barracks."

"To inspect Army barracks! And why, may I ask?" replied the Governor testily.

"Cholera!" was Dr. Walls's simple reply.

"Cholera? Among the soldiers?"

"Yes," asserted Dr. Walls.

Without a word the Governor summoned an aide and spoke a few words to him. Within minutes, the following permission was handed to Dr. Walls with the Governor's official seal:

BY ORDER OF THE GOVERNOR
Dr. Walls and his staff have special permission to enter the barracks of the Army of His Majesty King Edward and to subject any soldier to a medical examination. It is incumbent upon all Army personnel to cooperate fully with Dr. Walls and his staff.

Having taken the official paper, Dr. Walls was eager to depart, but the Governor interrupted him, "Is there anything else you need?"

Dr. Walls stopped short in his tracks at this query and immediately answered, "I would like this news to be communicated urgently to London. We need hospital equipment, beds, doctors, nurses…"

The Governor, who did not want to miss such an opportunity, immediately approached his royal guest, Lord Hamilton, and apprised him of the woeful news about the army.

Lord Hamilton offered to personally dictate the telegram in his name, which would produce a swifter reaction from London, and inquired if there was something else he could do to help. The Governor, who smelt a unique opportunity, asked his royal guest to release one million pounds sterling for this emergency. Lord Hamilton complied without hesitation. With this worthy acquisition in hand, the doctors took their leave.

Dr. Desquin was much impressed with Dr. Walls's insistence on getting a job done. To add icing to the cake, on their way back to the hospital Dr. Walls told Dr. Desquin of the other things that the Governor would send to the hospital.

Dr. Desquin concluded, "At least we have enough saline water."

"Well, that's one theory. There are other theories. Personally, I don't believe in anything unless we have the right drug to cure the infected people. My only concern right now is to limit the spread of this ugly disease."

Dr. Desquin, to whom a word from Dr. Walls was law, ventured, "We need more manpower."

"That is the least of my concerns. We need firewood for the cremations."

"For the Europeans too?"

"I am not concerned about the Europeans right now. They will be the least affected. And after all, they are used to seeing cremations here."

"And what about John?" lamented Dr. Desquin.

"Now that's another story. I believe he is in a deep coma," was Dr. Walls's clinical reply.

Dr. Desquin felt that the cholera problem would erase the recent bad impression that he had left on Mr. Mershenson, and with Dr. Walls at his side he could see his image in society improve considerably. After all, if there were to be thousands of dead, John's problem would be relatively small. Such was the train of his thoughts.

Sonia had spent the night listening to Mr. de Montaigne talk about John. When he began to tell her about Josephine and John on board the ship, she felt a seed of jealousy spring in her mind, but was soon sorry to be thinking of herself while John lay unconscious in the hospital. Finally, the exhausted girl fell asleep on a sofa. Mr. de Montaigne understood her feelings and was saddened. He spent the entire night in the library, waiting for daylight.

In the small hours before dawn, the Governor

called Dr. Walls to ask for the name of his liaison man. Without hesitation, Dr. Walls answered, "Dr. Desquin." The Governor was taken aback, "But he is a Frenchman!"

"No, he is British, born in Pondicherry, the French colony."

"I have no intention of designating a Frenchman in this matter. It might provoke a political problem, something I'd rather avoid."

At this, Dr. Walls replied, "There's a way to circumvent the matter. Call him Desqueen, if you like."

"Ha! That is a different question. So we shall change his name, Doctor! And I am sure Dr. Desquin will not object. The man seems to carry his name like a burden. Send him to me, and I will have his papers changed in a jiffy. I already have approval for a one million pound contingency fund."

On hearing this tidbit of news, Dr. Walls grinned to himself with vicarious pleasure. Now it remained for him to convince Dr. Desquin to change his name, so as not to jeopardize his entire operation. That should be easy.

Here was the realization of his dreams, something he had waited for, for more than five years. Dr. Walls had good reason to be pleased with himself.

As Dr. Walls was thus musing, the telephone rang again. It was the Governor's residence again, but this time it was His Lordship, the Right Royal Lord Hamilton, who wanted to have a word with Dr. Walls.

"The Governor just informed me about Dr. Desquin. You will of course make sure that no Frenchman finds out about this epidemic. We don't want a political problem on our hands, and you know the French are our Enemy Number One."

"My Lord, I can vouch for Dr. Desquin being one hundred percent British."

"Yes, but I am told his wife is French. Do you know what that means?"

"I do, My Lord, but I am not a politician after all, so I guess I shall limit myself to controlling the epidemic."

Lord Hamilton, fully aware of the political impact and the unrest that could ensue with news of the epidemic, replied, "Well, Dr. Walls, do your best and make sure to keep the newsmongers away from you. You know how those people can create a panic and cause us nothing but problems. I have to continue with the ceremonials this morning. After all, I am not here every day. Carry on as though nothing has happened."

"Yes, My Lord, I understand. Though, we can hide everything but the dead."

"Have them cremated by night. I shall instruct the Governor to give you all the help you need."

While Lord Hamilton was thus speaking on the phone to Dr. Walls, the Governor was seated beside him. Both gentlemen walked out together from the office. Upon seeing them, Lady Hamilton turned to her husband, saying "Darling, I want to see more of India!"

The Governor answered in good form, "My Lady, today you shall see how glad the Indians are to have us here."

To this, Lady Hamilton answered, "I certainly hope so. They would starve without us and probably kill each other with all their differences between religions and tribes. After all, it is we who gave them food, work, education and health." The Governor winced at Her Ladyship's last word, but managed to keep his smile intact.

John was still in a coma. He dreamed about Sonia and Josephine. Decades later, when he celebrated his sixtieth birthday, this dream came back to him. While he was in a coma, which no one expected him to recover from, he dreamed of Sonia, who gave him stability, confidence and happiness, and of Josephine, who had given him love. He had to struggle within himself. He knew that he had to choose between them. He would have preferred to have them both, but he knew that this was impossible and could only happen in the Arabian Nights, where men could have more than one wife. He could see nothing wrong with this Middle Eastern way of life. But he knew that he had grown up in a European society that had different rules.

CHRISTINA

When John finally opened his eyes, a young nurse was sitting next to him. John did not realize what had happened to him. "Where am I?" he mumbled.

Christina, the young nurse, answered, "Hush! Be still. You are in good hands."

John fell asleep again and had strange dreams. When he next woke up, he recognized Christina. He began to speak to her in English, forgetting completely that he was French. While he could see he was in a hospital, he had no recollection of what had happened to him. "Where are we?" he asked weakly.

"In India," replied Christina, who had prayed for him ever since he came to the hospital. She helped him sip some soup, which he took with relish. He seemed to be recovering from the shock, but Christina had no idea about his past. When she saw that John was able to talk clearly, she felt she had to tell him about Sonia. "You know, John, Sonia was here for hours, sitting at your bedside."

"Sonia? Who is Sonia?" asked John.

"Your friend with whom you went horse-riding."

"I have never ridden a horse, and I don't remember any friend," said John irritably. Christina realized that John was not yet recovered entirely from the shock and wisely refrained from pursuing the subject.

John continued the conversation. "How long have you been in India?"

"Three years," said Christina.

"Three years," repeated John and dozed off.

Sonia arrived a moment later hoping to find John awake. She saw Christina and asked her about John. Christina told her that John had been awake for a few moments and that he seemed to be recovering fast, but she refrained from telling her about John's loss of memory. Sonia waited for almost two hours, sitting by his bed and gazing at his handsome face. He looked well. That reassured Sonia. Then, after a while, she went home, leaving a message with Christina to tell John, when he woke up, that she would visit him and that she loved him dearly.

Mr. de Montaigne, who had accompanied Sonia to the hospital, was overjoyed to hear that John had awakened from his coma. He did not want to disturb him and went with Mr.

Mershenson to speak to the doctors, but neither Dr. Desquin nor Dr. Walls was to be reached, and after a long wait they took Sonia home.

A few hours later, John awoke again. Christina was just passing by his bed and was happy to see his face radiant with happiness and quite oblivious of all that had happened. She sat down companionably by his bed, and John repeated, "You have been in India for three years!" Christina was amazed that John had remembered her last remark before he fell asleep.

She replied, "Yes, I have been here for three years, and since you were brought here you have made me see my purpose in life. I know that you love Sonia."

John, on hearing the word "Sonia", repeated, "Sonia? You must be joking. I have only known her for a few moments, here in the hospital. I thought she was a nurse."

"No, she is not a nurse. She must love you so much; she was here so many times, sitting by your bed."

John was surprised and continued, "Why me?"

"You were together when you fell off the horse."

"What horse are you talking about?"

Christina realized that John still had problems with his memory and changed the subject in order not to upset him. But John wouldn't give up. "I fell off a horse, but I don't remember a horse. I must be here because of the cholera!" He then saw the bandage on his arm, which he had never noticed before, and asked Christina how this injury came about. He tried to find a connection between the wound and the horse, and every time he tried to connect the two factors he felt a sense of dizziness and felt his vision blur. He shut his eyes tightly to avoid the nauseating sensation. Christina saw him struggle with distress. She could not understand what was going through his mind. She kept telling him to relax and sleep, but he did not want to give up these troubling thoughts.

In an effort to break his train of thought, she repeated, "John, ever since you came here, your presence has given me a sense of purpose in life."

John looked at her with his deep, thoughtful eyes. He had fleeting thoughts of a romance but was too weak to concentrate on any subject. He answered politely, "Thank you for your kind words." Christina saw that the change of subject had relaxed him. His face was handsome in repose. She decided that she must tell Sonia that he had not quite recovered from the shock and that she must abstain from visiting him and let him recover slowly and take the time necessary in such a situation. She acted with John's best interests at heart and with no other motive.

Dr. Walls and Dr. Desquin were happy that John was recovering, but neither had realized the new complication that Christina had just experienced with John. Both doctors were so busy with the epidemic that the fact that John was alive was consolation enough for them.

Christina tried to explain about the cholera to John, but his mind kept wandering to the horse and the wound. He could see no correlation. He finally fell asleep in a troubled state of mind.

A week passed by in much the same manner, but youth and a strong constitution were on his side, and John began to recover rapidly. Soon he began to notice that there was a great deal of activity going on in the hospital. Christina had limited her duties to taking care of John and a few other patients. John's mind gradually became clearer. While he did not remember the past, the present was very clear to him.

Sonia, after the discussion she had had with Christina, had taken her request seriously and had abstained from visiting John for the past month. She called Christina daily, and Christina faithfully reported John's progress to her. All of his fractures had healed, to Dr. Walls's great satisfaction. John began to walk through the hospital freely. He had by now quite forgotten the story of the horse and Sonia.

Christina grew closer to him every day, as a friend, not a lover. She respected his intelligence and his education. John noticed with what diligence and devotion Christina worked. One day he decided that he would like to be useful to Christina and to the patients. He helped wherever he could. Dr. Walls and Dr. Desquin were pleased to see John help in such a critical situation. One day Christina requested John's help as she hurried about distributing clean sheets to the sick. John asked her for a set of sheets, so he could lessen her load. Christina laughed and said, "John, would you like to be a nurse?"

John turned serious at this question. He replied, "Christina, I know I have been sick, but that doesn't mean that I have forgotten my studies." Christina thought he was joking, when suddenly John began explaining to her in great detail and with medical terminology what cholera was. Christina was taken aback at his knowledge and his eloquence. She began to think that she really knew very little about John.

Dr. Walls appeared at this moment and, seeing them deep in serious medical discussion, said peremptorily, "We have a lot to do."

John replied, "I was just explaining something to Nurse Christina here, and it seems to me my explanation might be quite useful for all your nurses, as I see that they do not know too much about cholera, or about medicine at all for that matter."

Dr. Walls burst out laughing and said, "I'd rather you gave them a talk about love. That they need badly."

Christina was surprised to see the normally serious Dr. Walls so relaxed and jovial. To top it all, Dr. Walls's breath had a distinct smell of whiskey, something she had never noticed before. Dr. Walls, slightly unsteady on his feet, said to John with mock respect, "Professor John, do you think I could help you in your noble task?"

John answered seriously, "Certainly, Dr. Walls, as soon as you cease to be inebriated." Christina watched the goings-on between these two in silent amazement.

Dr. Walls continued, "Professor, do you think I could learn medicine?"

John continued in the same tone, "It is never too late Dr. Walls."

Dr. Walls, "Don't you think I am too old to begin to learn?

"Learning has no age limit," answered John, who began to explain to Dr. Walls how to limit the spread of cholera bacterium. Dr. Walls listened to John, this time with interest, despite the few pegs of whiskey that he had put away. He liked John and let him talk. First, he was pleased to see his patient, who had been so close to death, in good physical shape and thinking clearly. At this stage only Christina knew about John's loss of memory and was understandably concerned. Dr. Walls couldn't have noticed, and as he knew very little about John's romance, he didn't realize anything was out of the ordinary.

Christina wanted very much to speak privately to Dr. Walls about this, but she did not dare interrupt him. The chief doctor's cutting tongue was widely known and feared. Soon the doctor turned to Christina and remarked, "You do not seem to be enjoying our conversation, Sister."

Christina took a breath and answered, "Dr. Walls, I would very much like to discuss something with you."

Dr. Walls, with a short laugh, said, "You can talk to me now, and please don't tell me that you are in love with John."

Christina, seeing that Dr. Walls was not taking her seriously, was quiet and then said, "No, that is not the case, but it is something very important, and I would rather talk with you in private."

John seemed embarrassed by Christina's interruption. He politely excused himself and walked away. Dr. Walls was annoyed by this nurse, who was exceeding her duty. Turning to her he said in a clipped tone, "Now what is it you want to tell me?"

"John cannot recall his past."

"Are you out of your mind? I have never seen such a sharp memory. Did you not hear the way he spoke about cholera, which must come from his zoology lessons, or from reading? I will thank you to remember your position as a nurse and not try to diagnose my patients. Kindly leave that job to me. Do you understand?"

Christina felt the tears sting her eyes at this unnecessarily belligerent attitude of Dr. Walls and could barely answer. "Yes, Dr. Walls. I am sorry, sir." She hurried away to her duties.

Dr. Walls walked to his office muttering to

himself, "How stupid can a nurse be!" He was proud of his acuity. He had never had a discussion with Christina. He must have misjudged her in thinking her smart. Christina was a stupid nurse. Case closed.

When Dr. Desquin arrived at Dr. Walls's office, he was overwhelmed by the news of John's health. He was delighted and rushed to convey the glad tidings to his dear patient, Mr. Mershenson.

Sure enough, the very next day the entire Mershenson family, along with Mr. de Montaigne, paid John a visit. The visit was quickly cut short, as John did not recognize them and walked away without any explanation. Mr. Mershenson tried to calm Mr. de Montaigne and his own daughter by explaining that John must be angry over their absence and that they should stay calm and return the next day.

A few days went by, but Sonia's and John's father's visits were in vain. John was completely indifferent to their presence. They were like strangers to him. After over a month of daily visits from Sonia and Mr. de Montaigne, both stopped visiting.

Meanwhile, the epidemic was taking its toll. John was absorbed in his preoccupation with the sick. The hospital had become a part of him. He never cared about or looked after himself. His main concern was to keep the nurses on their toes. One day, Christina complained of a headache. John immediately sensed that she was overwhelmed with work and on the verge of a nervous breakdown. He ordered her to go home and rest. Christina, aware of her enormous responsibilities, did not want to go home. John became angry and repeated, somewhat impatiently, "Go home, Christina!"

Christina, too exhausted to argue with John, decided to go home. Before leaving, however, she asked John, "Will you visit me tonight?"

"Yes, I will," answered John without paying any thought to the matter. Christina was happy and left for home.

She slept all afternoon. As dusk deepened, John remembered his promise to Christina and prepared to visit her at home. This was John's first visit to the outside world after his admittance to the emergency room several months earlier. He rummaged in his pocket and found the little piece of paper on which Christina had written her address and thoughtfully, as was her wont, had slipped it into his pocket. However, she had not remembered that John was new to Bombay and did not know his way about.

John walked out of the hospital compound and got into one of the many small cabs that were always waiting. Soon, after a short and shaky ride through cobbled streets and alleys, he reached Christina's home. He knocked on the door. No one answered. He tried to look in through the window but could see no light or sign of Christina. He had a feeling that maybe Christina had never reached her home but had fainted on the streets somewhere. He knocked again, harder and more insistently this time. Christina, who was deep in slumber, heard the door, and the last dregs of sleep disappeared from her eyes. She recalled having asked John to come over, sat up and without arranging her hair or changing out of her nightdress, ran to the door to let him in. John seemed relieved to see her. "Come in, John," said Christina shyly. John entered the room, which seemed pitch dark at first. Presently, his eyes got used to the darkness. There was also pale light streaming in through the open window from the street lamps.

Christina soon appeared holding a hurricane lamp in her hand. She set it down on a small side table and smiled at him. John was happy to see her smile and relieved that she was not ill, as he had feared.

He said, "I see you are tired. Go back to sleep, and I shall see you tomorrow at the hospital."

Christina seemed very put out at this. He saw her face fall. "But I thought you would have dinner with me." John realized that Christina needed him to be there and gave in to her insistence. He did remember how kind Christina had been to him during his recuperation. He felt that it was now his turn to be helpful to her. He pulled up a chair and sat down. Christina suddenly became aware of her flimsy nightgown and slipped off to her bedroom to change into a pretty dress.

John had never seen Christina dressed in civilian clothes before. He had always seen her dressed in a nurse's uniform. He now looked at her sitting across from him at the table and was struck by her beauty. He somehow felt that he owed her a great deal but demurred from making any compliments for fear of giving her false hopes. Until now he had looked upon her as a friend. He had never thought of her as a woman. He looked at her eyes, and they expressed a stillness that was appealing to him. She sat quietly content in his presence.

THE SPIDER'S WEB

John felt embarrassed at this intimate silence and was the first to break it. He began, "Christina, I have known you now for more than two months and I still do not know anything about you. Tell me about yourself, your life. Why have you come to India? You are so young. You should be married and maybe have a child or two."

At these words, Christina burst into tears. John thought he might have said something to hurt her. He took her hand and said, "Christina, did I say something to hurt you? I'm sorry."

Christina, her eyes brimming with tears, attempted a smile and, caressing his cheek with her soft hand, said, "No, my dear friend, you just told me the truth. I don't remember if I told you my story in the hospital. You were very sick then, but I shall tell you again."

She told him that she had loved a man when she lived in England. Her friend had had an accident in a game of polo. He never recovered and died a few months later. That was when she had decided to come to India and to dedicate her life to the sick. John listened closely to Christina. Then he said consolingly, "I know and understand your pain, but you must take care of yourself!"

Christina replied, "And of you, too!" John,

his mind absorbed by his own sick patients, did not notice her love for him and, sadly for Christina, took it as normal good relations.

A while later, John left Christina and returned to the hospital. As he walked through the streets, Bombay did not seem new to him. He knew every street and short-cut on his way back. The walk took him more than an hour. It was already late at night when he returned to the hospital.

Dr. Walls was still in his office, and John joined him. The two of them launched into an intimate conversation like old friends. They looked at each other and seemed to know what was in the other's mind. "Christina is a strange girl," said Dr. Walls.

"Yes, but we shouldn't have spoken in front of her," answered John.

Dr. Walls stared at John and said, "It is not easy for people to realize that we are one with each other. Everyone has a different body, whether old or young, but we are the same, like drops in the ocean. A drop of water in the ocean is still part of the ocean."

"I shouldn't have spoken to you in front of Christina," mused John.

"No, it is my fault," said Dr. Walls adamantly,

"I had had a peg too much to drink."

John continued, "When you called me 'Professor', I believed you."

Dr. Walls decided that the conversation was getting too involved, laughed lightly and said emphatically, "I was joking." Dr. Walls had a strange feeling that John had as much medical knowledge as he did. He also felt that John was not completely aware of this treasure trove of knowledge within him. He got up and stretched, "Well, I guess we have had enough of this doctor game for one day. We have a long day ahead tomorrow. There's so much to be done. Get some rest. I need your help tomorrow."

Dr. Walls was pleased to discover John's abilities. He felt he could enlighten John with a few discussions about his inherent abilities and that John could finally save them from the cholera epidemic.

John walked out and came upon Dr. Desquin stretched out on an armchair, fast asleep. He walked on, saying to himself, "Everyone is fast asleep. If we could only awake from this long sleep and dream, we would be able to perform miracles." He glanced back once more and found Dr. Desquin in the same position. He walked back halfway towards him, then thought, "Poor man.

He must be exhausted." He continued walking towards his room, still murmuring to himself, "Better let him sleep. At least he won't have to see the people dying. When we sleep, we are not aware of the truth. It is only when we awake that we realize all the suffering around us. Closed eyes see nothing. Sleep on, Doctor. Don't hear the death cries and moans; it might just drive you mad." John fell into deep sleep on his bed and awoke early, ready to take on the world. His sense of responsibility was keenly developed.

Christina, too, arrived refreshed and ready to go to work. She found Dr. Desquin still asleep on the armchair and walked over to wake him up. As she gently shook him, he slipped further into the chair, and she realized with a sudden ache that he was dead. In fact, Dr. Desquin had been dead a long time. She realized that there are some people around us who are here only to help others and to save their fellow beings from misery. In reality, once their duty is fulfilled, they disappear or die. Christina recalled John's visit of the night before and thought to herself, "He must be one of those people." She felt, quite unjustifiably, that she had known John for years. She decided she would always stay with him, because she felt a sense of comfort and confidence in his presence

– she felt she was home, that her journey was over, whenever she was with him. She watched him, and over him, diligently. It was her earnest desire to know the real John, John in action. She wanted to know his every mood and feeling.

From day to day John became, for Christina, the man she knew and loved best. But not a word passed her lips. The activity at the hospital became intense, and John labored on without a moment's relaxation. He helped wherever he could. Every nurse felt his uplifting presence. He was never tired. He never complained. Christina noticed that John was doing things that only a trained doctor could do. Everyone respected him, much to Christina's pleasure. He was there, a bastion of comfort for both the sick and the healthy. Christina knew that John had forgotten the past with his father and Sonia. He never spoke about them, never wondered how he had come to India. This environment and these people seemed part of him, as if he had been born here, as if he had never known any other world.

Christina was the only one who knew all that had happened to John, and she never confronted him with facts that he might find disturbing. She never reminded him about Sonia. She loved him whole-heartedly, but she was never overt about her love. She did it discreetly. To her, John was a miracle-worker. The number of dead began to diminish from day to day. While no real drug was available to treat the sick or curtail the epidemic, the only simple solution that worked was devotion - keeping the patients clean and providing them with enough water, so that they did not die of dehydration. A solution made of unrefined brown sugar and salt that the natives used for cooking seemed to work wonders.

John's name was on every sick person's lips. The word "John" in several Indian languages meant "life", and he seemed the very embodiment of it. Time did not have any dimension for John. All that mattered was that he should be able to help. Christina wondered who would have kept down the death toll, if not for John.

No one knew who John was and where he came from. They knew only that he was the guest of Mr. Mershenson, who came daily to see him. John never acknowledged his presence. He was civil, and that was all. Sonia was in despair, but more in love with John than ever for his selfless devotion to the sick. John attributed Mr. Mershenson's visits to a nobility of character. Sonia's feelings were a mixture of guilt and love. Her heart was always attracted to John. She felt a fire in her heart every time her eyes met John's. So many thoughts of ill-boding passed through her mind. Her visits to the hospital became more and more frequent, just so she could be in John's presence. John's indifference did not discourage her; on the contrary, she loved him all the more.

One day Mr. Mershenson came upon a tearful Sonia in her room. He tried in vain to comfort her and calm her down. For two days in a row, Sonia stayed in her room without a bite to eat. Her father brought in another doctor to examine her. The doctor could see nothing wrong with her. He suggested that Sonia probably needed a change, perhaps a vacation might help, somewhere in Europe. "You need to relax, my dear. You are tired and exhausted," said the doctor in a patronizing voice.

At these words, Sonia sprang up from her bed in a burst of nervous energy and said, "I am not tired! I want to work in the hospital and help however I can. There are sick people here who need help much more than I need a rest."

The doctor was flabbergasted. "Do you know what you are saying? You may get infected with cholera. Your constant visits to the hospital have already put you at high risk."

To this Sonia answered, "And you, Doctor,

you are in the hospital every single day. Aren't you putting yourself at risk too?"

"My dear young lady, this is my profession and my duty," declared the doctor.

"And just your duty?" said a very belligerent Sonia. "It is everyone's duty and specially my duty," and Sonia emphasized her point by stamping her foot, a feature of the famous Mershenson temper.

Mr. Mershenson looked at this new version of his daughter with surprise, and at the pompous doctor's discomfort with secret amusement. He wondered if he should really take the doctor's advice and send Sonia away. But he never did really want her to be far away from his side. She had already been deprived of her mother. Should he now deprive her of her father too?

Sonia was calm now. She said determinedly, "I will work in the hospital, whether you like it or not." Mr. Mershenson agreed in powerless despair.

That day John worked all day without a break and without a bite to eat. He collapsed on the bed of a sick man who had just expired. Christina saw this happen. She fetched Dr. Walls immediately, and John was wheeled away to the operating room. When Dr. Walls emerged from the theatre, Sonia had arrived and was waiting. The scene was just as it had been on the first day. Dr. Walls greeted Sonia, who felt her heart beat uncomfortably fast. She had a premonition that something was wrong. Soon after, Christina, accompanied by another nurse, wheeled out a stretcher. Sonia could not make out who the patient was. Besides, Christina did not greet her with her usual sweet smile, but continued on her way with the nurse.

Sonia entered the large private room where she had always found John. She looked around; there was no sign of him. She could now feel her heart wrench with anguish. She got hold of herself, however, and went up to Christina, who had just laid John down on a bed. She called out, "Christina!"

Christina turned her head slowly, wondering how she would break the news to Sonia. She led Sonia to the waiting room, saying, "Sonia, I want to speak to you where we won't hear the moans of the dying." Sonia sensed that something had happened to John. She prayed that he would still be alive. Then she thought that maybe Christina wanted to tell her something else about John, and hope raised its welcome head.

Christina looked for a long time at Sonia.

Sonia found the suspense unbearable. She tried to calm herself. Christina must be under immense stress, with people dying all around her. The epidemic had taken a toll in more than lives, she thought. Christina tried to get a grip on herself. Sonia, at this point, was prepared to fight for John's life, if need be. She had to be with John at any price. She accepted in her heart that even if John did not recognize her, even if he was in love with someone else, it would not change her attitude. Her love was beyond John's love. She loved him for himself, and even if he belonged to someone else, it did not matter. She wanted to see him healthy and happy at all costs.

Suddenly, Christina, who also loved John selflessly, fell sobbing into Sonia's arms. Sonia tried to calm her and find out what was the matter. Christina was incoherent and crying with exasperation. The situation made Sonia realize that she had a steel strength that would carry her through. She held Christina tightly in her arms and patted her head till her sobs subsided. Finally she spoke.

"Our beloved John is ill. He passed out today, and Dr. Walls does not know why."

"Where is John?"

"He is still unconscious. We just have to

wait and see."

Sonia was mistress of herself and her feelings now. She knew her intuition was correct. From now on, she would be guided by her own feelings and not by what others said. Sonia realized that we are all interconnected, and that the most important thing in life is to love and not to hate. She loved her father, she loved Mr. de Montaigne, she loved John, she loved her teacher, she loved Christina, and she loved Dr. Desquin, who had just passed away. She realized that she loved everyone, and that this love gave her strength and wisdom. Although she had been deprived of her mother's love, her mother was alive in her heart, and she derived her vitality from that source. Christina looked up into Sonia's austere face and wanted to open up to her. She then explained to her the recent events. When she had finished, Sonia said, "Let us pray together for John and for everyone who needs help."

"I have loved John ever since he came to this hospital," Christina blurted out.

Sonia's reaction was to kiss her. "I am happy someone else could love John with all her heart and soul, as I do."

Sonia now became a part of the hospital.

It was hard to resist her determination to help. She was given a nurse's uniform and looked as though she had been made for it.

John awoke the next day, walked up unaided to the hospital office, and asked to be connected with Mr. Mershenson. Christina came upon John's empty bed on her daily rounds, advised Sonia, and both young women went out in search of him. Finally, they found him in the hospital office, waiting for a car to pick him up and take him to the Mershenson's. Upon seeing Sonia, he exclaimed, "Why, Sonia, you are here already!"

Sonia was overwhelmed with joy. "Oh, my love, how do you feel?"

"Fine," said John, without hesitation. They fell into each other's arms with abandon. Both Christina and Dr. Walls looked upon this wonderful scene with full hearts and slowly moved away, to leave the couple to themselves.

A while later, Christina felt that she could interrupt her friends and, smiling with happiness, entered the room. "How do you feel, John?" she asked.

John looked at her as if he was seeing her for the first time. All he could remember was that he was with Sonia and the horses. He looked blankly at Sonia and asked her, "Do you know this nurse?"

"Yes," said Sonia, "She nursed you back to health!"

John politely said, "I thank you for your kind services, dear lady, but honestly, I do not remember seeing you." Christina, without a word, slipped away from the office to be alone. This was the happiest day of Sonia's life.

Mrs. Desquin, who had suddenly become widowed, now got even closer to Josephine, who had meanwhile lost her own father. He had left her a fortune. Her only dream was to find her beloved John. She knew that he must be somewhere in India but had not the least idea that Dr. Desquin had been his physician. The two women spent their time consoling each other. They were close, despite their difference in age, and became like mother and daughter. Mrs. Desquin tried to create a connection between her son, who was studying in Europe, and Josephine. While Josephine did not completely oppose the idea as an alternative, she still wanted to make an effort to find John.

THE TEA BUSINESS

Mr. de Montaigne had in the meantime sailed for Europe to sell the tea that his friend had promised him. Mr. Mershenson's only way to compensate his friend for the tragedy that had befallen him was to give him the deal that he had wanted so badly. His first letter from Europe, which took two months to arrive, indicated that he had been quite successful and that he would like Mr. Mershenson to give him exclusivity for Europe. Mr. Mershenson, too busy with his daughter and John, and no longer concerned for his friend, did not write back.

Dr. Walls came upon a tearful Christina and took her to a room, gave her a sedative to relax her, and put her to bed. She slept all that day and into the next.

John asked Sonia to give him the details of his accident. He asked about Sonia's father, and finally about his own father. When he heard that his father had left for Europe, he felt quite bereft.

Mr. Mershenson arrived with much pomp in a new car, a "horselesss carriage", that he had

had specially imported from England. It was new and shiny, and he was very proud of it. He was thrilled to see the ecstatic faces of his daughter and John, as the last few months had been a test of his endurance. He now imagined that the dream of his lifetime would come true. After all, Sonia loved John, the son of his best friend and business partner. His fortune could be safely left in their hands. Sonia, relaxed at last, smiled on seeing her father, and taking John's hand, said, "Let's go home, father."

Mr. Mershenson was only too happy to oblige and led them to the car. John noticed the fine new car and was happy that he would not have to be squeezed in as on his first trip. The chauffeur opened the door for John with a majestic flourish, but John was mindful of his manners and with a "Ladies first," ushered Sonia in. She gathered up her long skirt in her hand and swept gracefully in. John followed. Mr. Mershenson, who was thrilled with his new possession and never tired of its complex workings, got in beside the giant Sikh chauffeur, so that he could satisfy his own curiosity about how the car worked.

John, who had never ridden in a car before, marveled at the noise, the steering, and the loud horn that made the pedestrians jump, and the thick, comfortable leather cushions. They sped along in a world of their own, smiling from time to time at each other, as if they had all just met. A sense of happiness and joy enveloped them, and the car added to the festive atmosphere. Mr. Mershenson was happy too, but absorbed in exploring the new car's buttons and mechanisms, which his chauffeur indulgently explained to him.

They relaxed as the noisy trappings of the bustling city fell behind them. The road was pleasant and John looked out at the greenery passing them by, which he had not seen on his first journey. Suddenly, a sense of grief filled his heart at the absence of his father. Everything would have been perfect, if only his father had been here. He tried to console himself by thinking that soon his father would be back from Europe.

John loved Sonia so much that he dedicated his time to helping Mr. Mershenson with his business papers. He visited the spot where he had had the accident, accompanied by Sonia. Sonia never again mentioned horses. In time, John became quite an expert in the tea business, so much so that Mr. Mershenson, during the very next year, doubled his profits. John was reliable and he had everything he wanted, including

Sonia.

Mr. Mershenson realized that the domestic situation was becoming rather embarrassing, as it was generally known that John and Sonia were living together, and he would have liked to formalize the relationship with a marriage and his blessing, but Mr. De Montaigne's absence kept him from resolving this delicate problem. He decided to finally write to his friend and apprise him of the situation.

He never received an answer to his letter. Months later, he met a merchant who had just arrived from France and had known Mr. de Montaigne. He informed Mr. Mershenson about the sad demise of Mr. de Montaigne. The news left Mr. Mershenson desolate, but he abstained from announcing the news for a few weeks to John and Sonia, so as not to mar their happiness, since they were in Seventh Heaven, and also so as not to endanger his business, as John had become indispensable to his business. John had become a very astute businessman; Mr. Mershenson had not seen such keen insight for years. He decided to shelve the idea of a marriage for the present and let things be. John was deeply involved in his job and very loyal to him. John's main concern was to protect the Mershenson business and make it prosper from day to day.

Christina had suddenly turned religious, not by conviction, but by deception, so as to be able to see John from afar, aware that he had forgotten her. She dedicated her life to Christ. The Son of God now took John's place in her heart, yet whenever she saw John in the city, she felt lonely and miserable, even towards Jesus. She could not help it; she loved both of them. She could not understand why it was wrong to love a man like John, and why the Son of God should mind. After all, love was Christ's main strength. She finally came to a compromise. She realized she had the right to love anyone, as long as she did not hate anyone. Despite all her reasoning, she was unhappy. She consoled herself thinking that at least John was alive, even though he was living with Sonia. There was a kind of poetic justice to it; after all, Sonia had loved him first, and as long as John was happy, she would be happy too. She loved him so much; it was far beyond mere physical love. She remembered Sonia's patience when John had lost his memory. Strangely enough, as John recovered, the cholera epidemic had also receded, as if God was pleased with John. Now and then there were single cases, and each one of them survived. Christina's duties became less onerous as the epidemic abated.

The situation only made her more lonely and sad. She did her best not to disturb John's happiness with Sonia. But matters only got worse, and she began to spend sleepless nights. All her thoughts were concentrated on John. She saw all her hopes and desires dashed through his absence. She seemed to have been born to suffer for the hospital. She tried her best to be serene, but without success. Her love had turned into a sickness. She did her best to forget him, but every time she saw him, she turned melancholic. She now wanted to fight the Earth and the Sky, God and His Son. Unhappy thoughts occupied her mind. She felt that the only way to regain her peace was to do away with her miserable existence. She knew that even if she left India, John would not leave her heart. She could not share her grief and suffering with anyone.

One day, she awoke calm and balanced. After all, John and Sonia knew nothing about her suffering and her love. They deserved kindness. She would send them flowers. Then again, the next day, her feelings underwent a change, and she felt the same way as when she had lost her friend in London. Her unhappiness did not pass unnoticed at the hospital. She had lost her sense of mission and her reason for coming to India. Her heart now burned with a warmer flame. Many a time she ran to the hospital's storeroom to cry her heart out.

Dr. Walls, who had started to appreciate her services, was concerned when he came upon her crying one day. He, a lonely bachelor, had begun to fall in love with her. He tried to court her, very tactfully and patiently, but without success. She did not even notice his change of attitude. She noticed him no more than a blind person notices the beauty of a flower.

Dr. Walls, who spent so much tenderness and patience on Christina, could not understand why she did not respond to his love. He had begun to feel worn out from the exhausting schedule and the sheer weight of his work. For the first time in his life, it was not enough to be a renowned doctor. He was lonely. He realized that he had spent his entire youth helping others. He felt it was time he spared a few thoughts for himself. He had never had a family or a real friend. He felt Christina would be the one to give him a sense of purpose in life. He had never realized the depth of Christina's suffering.

Dr. Walls, the epitome of respect and the object of envy, began to decline. He had bouts of memory loss. In fact, there were even times when he prescribed the wrong medicine. Christina noticed this, but attributed it to his long days at the hospital. She could not imagine that his love for her had made him lose his focus. One never thinks that a strong person may need the love, the warmth, and the care of others. One expects the leader only to give. But in reality, as in the case of Dr. Walls, the strong also need someone to take care of them.

Dr. Walls, who possessed a keen intellect, had noticed these lapses in his memory. He wondered how a man like him could get into such a state. He did not press Christina for a commitment, but suffered silently. The invincible Dr. Walls, who had been able to defeat the epidemic, was now helpless in the face of his feelings towards Christina. Here were two persons, both eager for love, but suffering next to each other. Months passed, but nothing happened to allay the burning fire in the heart and mind of Dr. Walls for Christina, and in Christina for John.

Dr. Walls, a tower of strength who could resolve the most complex problems, was now defenseless when touched by love. He realized the strength of love. He realized why even the strongest man could be troubled where his feelings were concerned. He thought to himself, "This is as it should be. We are all equal, poor or rich, academic or illiterate. We all have the same feelings when it comes to love or distress." He concluded that if he could not have Christina's love, he would be content simply with her presence at the hospital. The most important thing was that she was alive. He hoped his feelings would change with time. He knew from his studies that time was an important healing factor. Our hearts can suddenly be enlivened on a bright, sunny day, and be heavy again on a cloudy day. We can control many things, but we are helpless when it comes to our feelings. Although he had studied the science of the human body, he had never studied the science of feelings. When our feelings, good or bad, overcome us, we become helpless. Those who have never experienced these feelings are not human. Time can heal many wounds. Maybe a change of scene and atmosphere would bring Christina close to him.

John, who had become the pillar of Mr. Mershenson's fortune, and whose responsibilities increased from day to day, spent all his time travelling on business and in the office. Gradually he began to spend less and less time with Sonia.

THE SPIDER'S WEB

He was frequently absent. She plunged into loneliness and spent most of her time in her room. She began to suffer, too. Mr. Mershenson, however, was ecstatic. He loved John and depended entirely on him. He had little time for Sonia and was proud to have John as a potential son-in-law. John, to show his love for Sonia and to return her father's kindness, devoted his entire time to increasing Mr. Mershenson's fortune. It was not that he had any other romantic interest, but this was his way of showing how much he loved her. To Sonia, however, this devotion to work meant little. She wanted him close to her and to spend his time cherishing her. She had had enough of her father's fortune. She did not realize that John and her father wanted her happiness and neither wanted her to lack anything in life. The two men were realistic, but Sonia could not understand their way of thinking.

Every time Sonia visited John's office, it was always, "Later, my love, I am very busy right now." He reasoned that once he was firmly positioned and had enough money, he would have all the time in the world to cherish his beloved Sonia. He explained this to her, but his explanation was entirely unsatisfactory to her. She became resentful of her father's and of

John's preoccupation with work. Everyone was lonely and sad except Mr. Mershenson, who was delighted and had no notion that his precious daughter was very unhappy, and would have been quite willing to sacrifice his life for her if need be.

John wanted to make everyone happy, but the opposite was the case. John was quite unaware that he was the cause of two broken hearts. He did reminisce about Josephine once in a while, but he had not heard from her for ages, and he didn't feel responsible for her.

Christina in the meantime had finally realized that Dr. Walls was deeply in love with her, which explained his change of attitude towards her, and his kindnesses and thoughtfulness. She became very careful about anything she said to him. Anything he said received a careful analysis before she responded. She did not want to give him false hope and realized that he must be suffering as much as she was.

On one occasion John had to go for a survey of the tea gardens and live for a week in the overseers little bungalow, without the comforts that he had grown so used to. He never complained. He was happy to take the extra trouble for Sonia and her father. Sonia's love gave him a great deal of strength and endurance. She, however, was unhappy at John's absence. She wanted him for herself. She never realized that love involved a great deal of responsibility and obligation. She had never undergone any hardships, never known what the lack of money or food meant.

John had no inkling of what was going on in Sonia's mind. He noticed her change of attitude, which he attributed to her concern for his well-being. When he returned from his trip, he was drained with fatigue and did not notice that Sonia's look was different from her usual look. He slept through the entire day. The day after, during breakfast, Sonia smiled as usual, but did not give him a kiss, which went unnoticed by John.

From day to day, Sonia's indifference began to slowly catch his attention. Since he loved her and was happy that she loved him just as much, he was not unduly concerned. Sonia began going out and frequently staying out late. At first, John thought that Sonia was just lonely and was happy that she was going out shopping. After a week, he was worried and wanted to ask her where she was going, but the idea of doubting her loyalty was repugnant to him. He decided it would be insulting for him to question her sincerity

The week after, Sonia was still frequently absent from home. This time, John, who was never jealous, sensed that something was wrong with Sonia. He waited up for her in the trellised verandah that ran along the house. Sonia returned late. He did not like to think that she was having an affair with another man. He felt that she was too honest to seek the affections of another man, especially since she knew that he loved her, and that the time he spent away from her was not spent in trifling matters, but for her father and herself. He questioned her casually about the late hour, but she was a picture of wide-eyed innocence, and he was embarrassed at ever having doubted her loyalty and her love.

John saw that Sonia was no longer sad or discontented; in fact, she was quite pleasant and looked happy and smiled more than usual. She no longer fretted about the long hours John spent at work. They spent that night together, tenderly, like old times. Her passionate ardor had succeeded in dispelling any doubts from John's mind. She did look different, but John attributed this to the fresh air.

The following week, she continued to go out alone, and John was again perplexed. But every night on her return she succeeded in reassuring him. He felt stirrings of jealousy in his heart. One night, while they were both awake in bed, he asked her bluntly, "Sonia, are you seeing another man?" Sonia was indignant and demanded how he could ever think such an absurd thing. John was ashamed and relieved at the same time. He turned over and went to sleep.

Despite all of Sonia's assurances, John had a niggling feeling of doubt that just would not go away. He spent his entire day with painful thoughts of betrayal. He was in no mind to work. Sonia saw John's discontent and spent the whole next day with him, until it was quite late. She kissed him goodnight and stepped into the next room. John fell asleep but awoke suddenly, his heart racing. He dressed and walked out through the French door to get a breath of fresh air. The night air was cool and fragrant with flowers. It was almost two o'clock in the morning. His glance fell on a lighted window. It was Sonia's room. Maybe she had gone to sleep with the light still on. He decided to go into Sonia's room and turn off the light quietly.

He stepped over the gravel under the window and suddenly felt his hair stand on end. Two shadows fell across the heavy silk curtains.

His heart was thumping in agony now, but he was already too close to them. He surprised Sonia in the arms of a man he had never seen before. Sonia was defiant. She was neither ashamed nor embarrassed.

John left immediately without a word and paced the garden until dawn broke out in pale streaks across the horizon. Sonia realized her folly and that she had wounded John savagely. With it came the realization that she loved John more than anyone else. She had only meant to make him jealous, so that he would want her more. She did not want to lose him. But John had reacted in quite the opposite way. Sonia was now embarrassed and asked to be left alone. Then she cried like a child and spent an unhappy and sleepless night.

The 'other' man, who had only been used as bait, felt justifiably insulted and spent the rest of the night on a cold stone bench.

John was confused and disappointed. The sight of Sonia with another man stirred strange feelings in his heart. He thought he was prepared for anything, but that Sonia would hurt him was beyond his comprehension. He was no longer at peace with himself. He cursed the day he came to this country, a country that had caused him more suffering than he had experienced when he was little. He wanted to fight the Hindu Gods. He just could not overcome the pain. He saw his dreams and future washed away like a sandcastle at high tide. He became listless and apathetic from one day to the next.

Sonia couldn't find peace or happiness any more than John. Every time she saw the other man, she trembled with guilt and shame. He ended up by abandoning her friendship. He was saddened and could not understand why he had been used in this shameful way. Sonia had never meant to betray John, because she really loved him deeply, but in her young, thoughtless manner she had thought of awakening his love by making him jealous, so that he would give up his excessive dedication to building her father's fortune, and so that he would love her all the more. But neither the absence of the other man nor Sonia's loneliness could repair the harm done. John felt that Sonia had hurt him deeply and betrayed his trust. Nothing could heal his disappointment or his wound.

Now, John began to search for something real, something pure. He remembered the old man whom he had seen in the field on the day he arrived. His eyes and presence had given him a sense of peace and serenity. He wished that he had never met Sonia. He searched for the old man. The more John's thoughts were directed towards the old man, the more he felt at peace with himself. A sense of resignation filled his heart.

He neglected his work and wanted to destroy all that he had done, in order to appease the gods of his wrath. He could not see where all this was leading him. He wished he could find a solution that would set his heart at peace. He could not comprehend how a mature man, with all his wisdom and education, could be so much at the mercy of his feelings.

John began to understand that the more capacity he had to love, the more was his capacity to endure pain. He also understood that if he had the force to hate, he must also have the force to love. These various contradictory feelings disturbed him night and day, and he struggled with the dilemma of how to resolve these feelings. He decided that he had to first understand the meaning of each feeling. Explanations and education were not enough to understand this new language, the language of feeling which we ignore in our daily life and in our education. John began to realize how far modern society is from the life of feeling. He understood that the power of feeling is stronger than any other power. The power of feeling, when it captures our hearts, controls it completely and disrupts our normal life and our behavior. The only feeling that did not extract a toll from him was the feeling of happiness. On the contrary, it restored his complete conscience and clarity; it gave him complete freedom.

Now John had to analyze those feelings. And then again, the only feelings that could give him his freedom and happiness were the feelings he experienced with the old man. He did not know why. He decided to focus his energies on finding the old man and re-experiencing the feelings which brought him at peace with himself.

One day he would awake with a feeling of bitterness, and on another with love and peace; one day with the desire to work hard and build, and on another to destroy. He could not understand how a woman could so change the life of a man and maybe the life of another woman; how a woman could bring a man to the brink of despair; make him lose all sense of self-worth and self-respect. He could not understand how it was possible to be punished by someone whom he loved more than any other and to whom he had never done or wished any harm. It was he who had increased – and maybe saved – the fortune of Mr. Mershenson. How was it possible for his daughter to be so harsh towards him, to be so merciless and inconsiderate?

John remembered how his father had told him the story from the Bible about Adam and Eve. He remembered Eve had disobeyed God and had been tempted by the serpent. It was Eve who had infuriated God with her behavior. It was Eve who had deprived Adam of Paradise, and it was Eve who had brought down a world of suffering and contradiction on Adam. She had brought Adam into a world of conflicting forces and influences which he had to fight to survive. John could not imagine himself loving or trusting any other woman without reserve. How could he ever trust any other woman in the light of Eve's disobedience and disloyalty to God? Relying on a woman now seemed to John like being caught in a spider's web. From now on, the only way for him to go forward was to find a woman with whom he could have a life of harmony, a life with loyalty, with disregard to physical needs – a life of peace and happiness. John was now thinking about all aspects of life, trying to find the reason for his being here on Earth. He imagined a life of happiness could exist. The only way to find it was to first come to terms with himself, to awake and be aware of the various forces which directed his life.

John felt deep in his conscience that a human being made by God must be able to control all those various forces which existed within himself. Then he realized that no one could master anything without knowing and identifying each of those forces. The question was how to master them. He understood that a human being could live at the mercy of those forces and let them control his life at will. The only way to conquer them was first to come to a standstill. He tried to think how he could shut off his thoughts, even though that seemed very difficult. He realized that those forces could survive only if he gave them importance and consideration. The solution was to ignore his sufferings and all those feelings which had vanquished his mind and heart and body. He sensed that the day those forces could not play a role in his life, he would be himself. His instinct told him that once he had reached that stage, all those various forces would be at his mercy, and not vice versa. The way was long and full of pain and suffering, but it was the only way forward.

John recalled a circus in which he had seen all kinds of wild animals obeying the tamer. The tamer was in reality the master of all those wild animals, who obeyed him and did all he wanted them to do. If it was possible to train wild animals, it must be possible to train those feelings which made life miserable. The animal heart always needs a master to survive and to be happy. John concluded that those forces needed a tamer, and if they existed within himself, then he could be the only one to lead them. As these thoughts came to John, he felt his misery slowly dissipate, and this confirmed that his conclusion was the right one. Now it was up to him to be the leader and master of his own forces. Every human being can be his own leader, even though it is harder to tame one's own forces than to lead other people. An entire life may not suffice for this task. Its completion was the greatest achievement in life. An achievement such as this was greater than being the King of England. He wondered if even the King of England knew what he was doing. How could a king or leader lead other people if he had not achieved the noblest task within himself?

John started to realize that all sorts of wars and troubles in our world are the result of millions of uncontrollable wild forces. The world would never attain peace as long this task was not achieved by every human being. We are all interconnected, like it or not. And so long as these wild forces remained without control, they would continue to take their toll.

John recalled how he used to read from the Bible every night. His father had never spoken to him about those human feelings which agitate us and fling us about in different directions. He wondered if his father had had the same feelings and had learned to control them. But then he had never seen his father express unhappiness or change his attitude. He had always been serene and patient with John. He had never forced him to practice any religion, even though he read the Bible. He never tried to propagate any religion. John thought of the many missionaries whose main goal was to convert others. Had those missionaries converted these internal forces?

John tried to recall the face of the old Indian man who had made him so happy and so peaceful. Whenever he succeeded in recalling his face, the expression on the face was now different, one of anger. John wondered if the image he saw repeatedly had a meaning or a warning. He decided to go again into the fields and try to find the old man. He must see him, and this time, after two years in India, he would certainly understand his words. The first time he had been unable to understand anything. He had merely felt their impact. John wandered about for days looking for him. He was now familiar with every field and every path. After days of searching, he could not find the old man. He was in despair and wondered if he had dreamed it all up. Had the old man really existed, or was he just a figment of his imagination?

He might have doubted his eyes, but he could not doubt the feeling of serenity, happiness and generosity that he had experienced the day he saw the old man. It was hard to distinguish between the real and the unreal. He began to wonder if these were signs of a disturbed mind. He was confused. He had stopped thinking about Sonia. His main goal was to clarify the enigma of the old man. The only way he could regain his composure was to come to a conclusion. Either the old man existed or he did not. He continued his walks through the fields. He even spent a few nights in the fields, so as not to miss any chance of seeing him. When this produced no result, he began to check his memory, starting with the day he had left the vessel… day by day, minute by minute. He did not think any more about his father. In his mind, even when his father was alive, his absence had not bothered him. He was amazed that he did not have any feelings for the father whom he had loved so much. Nor did the memory of his mother mean anything to him. The only person who represented any meaning and a sense of nostalgia was the old man, whom he had seen for only a few minutes. It had been John's first encounter in India, and it had given him a sense of hope and life.

Mr. Mershenson had begun to be concerned about John and the business. The daily absences worried him. He never realized what had been going on between John and his daughter. John was his main concern, as he himself had lost touch with the business. Since John had started to take care of the business, Mr. Mershenson had stopped dealing with the details. He saw his business at risk.

BACK TO DUTY

Since John had left the hospital, Dr. Walls had become so absent-minded and committed so many errors, that he submitted his resignation one day, to the stupefaction of all who knew him. Christina continued her duty as usual, since this was the only thing that gave any meaning to her life. She had suffered from John's absence in the beginning, but gradually her dedication to her duty diminished her suffering. The hospital director hired a new physician to replace Dr. Walls. Christina remembered the day that Dr. Walls had been arguing with John and had called John 'Professor'. She wondered if Dr. Walls had been really drunk or had just been playing at being drunk. Suddenly, she decided to go and see John, even at the risk of upsetting Sonia. She had to find out what was going on between them.

Early that day, she rented a carriage and drove out to the Mershenson estate. She wandered about in search of John, at her wit's end and in despair. Suddenly, she realized that an old man was following her. She stopped and faced him. He apologized for interfering in her life and said, "The man you are looking for is in Mr. Mershenson's field. Let me show you the way." And he proceeded to mark a path for her in the dust with a twig. Christina listened to the old man without asking herself who he was and how he knew who she was looking for.

Christina took the path that the old man had described and felt renewed vigor. By early afternoon, she discovered John sitting cross-legged on the ground, lost in thought. He was unaware that he had company, until Christina said, "Professor, we have been looking for you for a long time!"

John did not even express surprise at the title and replied, "I'm sorry. I wanted to take a walk in the fields to get some air. I hope nothing untoward has happened in my absence from the hospital."

John stood up and walked back to the carriage with Christina. They both returned to the hospital. When they arrived, John picked up a white coat and began to diagnose the patients. He was sorry to have neglected them for the last few hours. He did not realize that he had been gone for months. Christina did not interfere with his work and gladly accepted his instructions.

She had no doubt that John was a real doctor, a master of medicine. She did not dare question his instructions, even though he was very young. In fact, John saved many patients whom Dr. Walls had considered beyond recovery.

John never spoke much. His main concern was the sick. He gradually gained a great deal of recognition. Surprisingly, no one asked him where he had studied. Even his doctor colleagues had tremendous respect for his abilities and judgment. A year passed by swiftly. John, unbeknown to himself, was very popular and admired. He had a faithful assistant in Christina, who never left his side.

News about John reached London and other European capitals. He lectured at various institutions on cholera and other waterborne diseases. His audiences admired his eloquence and his knowledge. John had complete confidence in himself and never doubted his abilities for a moment. Christina wept with joy whenever he gave a successful academic performance. She never spoke about her love to him. His presence alone was ample. She loved him more than anyone in the world. Her past became a nightmare that was soon erased from her memory.

Christina spent long days at the hospital.

She was tireless whenever she was working with John. He had forgotten Sonia and the Mershensons. John received many proposals to lecture at different universities but turned them all down. He used to say, "If they want to learn, let them come to the hospital." He never looked for merit or awards. His hospital became his castle and an integral part of him. His heart was light, and he was always happy. His exemplary attitude was a subject of pride to colleagues and nurses alike. He wanted nothing but to serve the sick. He was born to save lives. His look became similar to that of the old Indian man, deeply etched and exuding wisdom. He spoke only to the sick or to his colleagues, and always about how to alleviate pain.

Sonia now lived in sadness and despair, which she had herself created. She felt that she was punishing herself for having hurt John. He did not even recognize her anymore. She had wanted too much. She had not understood John's integrity and dedication. Her luck had slipped out of her hands like a slippery fish. Mr. Mershenson died in sadness and despair, leaving Sonia a fortune that only John knew how to manage.

John's walks in the hospital gardens became a daily habit and his only form of relaxation.

Christina always knew where to find him in case of an emergency. One day, John awoke early and walked towards the gardens. He saw the old man, for whom he had searched for so long without success. This time, the old man seemed to be waiting for him. They spoke in Hindi, of which John had picked up the rudiments and in which he was able to converse simply. The old man repeated the same words that John had been unable to understand the first time. They were, "Don't build your life on a spider's web." John experienced the same joy that he had felt the first time. He continued on his walk, full of understanding now, mature beyond his years. He never remembered his father or Mr. Mershenson. After a few steps, he turned again to look at the old man. The place was still the same, but the old man had disappeared, as if the earth had swallowed him up.

From that day on, John's faith and strength were unshakeable. He returned to the hospital, his eyes shining and full of joy. Everyone about him felt the joy of his presence.

Christina loved him wholeheartedly, but in quite a different way from Sonia. She loved him without demanding anything in return. She respected his freedom. She did nothing to attract him or to influence him. She loved him without any pretentions. The fact that John was in the hospital was enough to fill her heart with happiness. John gave her the purpose in life that she missed when he was with the Mershensons. Her mission in coming to India was clear now. She worked hard until the last patient was asleep. She never touched John or kissed him. She felt no need for these demonstrations of affection. Her love was wholly platonic.

Dr. Walls, who had long since left the hospital, suddenly returned. On his arrival, John, without any preamble, said to him, "Dr. Walls, could you take care of the other row of beds?" And Dr. Walls was back on his rounds. They spent hours together on research in the laboratory and discovered a number of drugs which eventually saved many lives. The hospital became famously known as 'John's Hospital'.

SONIA'S PLAN

Sonia realized that she could do nothing to change John. She decided to keep hold of him by means of her fortune. She was determined to have him, even if she had to kidnap him. She found his behavior unreasonable. She loved him, and he loved her, and that was reason enough for her to do what she was going to do. She visited the hospital regularly, but John was oblivious of her existence.

She then visited Mrs. Desquin, who had been very lonely since her husband's death. She was very charming to her and asked her if she could use her house to throw a party before her departure for America. Mrs. Desquin was only too happy to oblige. She remembered that the well-to-do Mershensons had been her husband's favorite patients. She felt honored that Sonia had considered her house for such an occasion. She had no inkling of Sonia's plans. Sonia requested that Mrs. Desquin be the host at her party and asked her to invite everyone she would like to see, including all the doctors at the hospital, especially Dr. Walls's young friend, as she herself would be too busy with preparations for her departure.

Mrs. Desquin spent the rest of the day sending out last minute invitations to one and all. Josephine gladly helped her with all her preparations. The entire medical community was happy to see Mrs. Desquin throw a party. While everyone had sympathized with her after her husband's death, they were wary of inviting her to social occasions, for fear of reminding her of her husband. On the few occasions that she had been invited, she had burst into tears.

Josephine had meanwhile given up all hope of finding John. She had married a rich man and had a lovely little daughter. Before his death, her father had told her the story of her mother, also called Josephine, who in fact had been Mr. de Montaigne's fiancée, but who had betrayed him and married another man years ago. That had been the underlying reason for Mr. de Montaigne's inexplicable dislike of the younger Josephine.

Sonia had taken all the necessary precautions. She had a passport issued in John's name through her influential relations, and she knew that the captain of the vessel had the authority to marry her to John.

That evening, Dr. Walls had hesitated to accept Mrs. Desquin's invitation but had finally agreed at Mrs. Desquin's insistence. He had also convinced John to accompany him. John had agreed only out of respect for Dr. Walls.

The Desquin residence was a picture of festivity and lights that evening. Strains of music floated out to greet the guests who had thronged to wish Sonia farewell. Most of the guests were prominent government officials, among them an officer of the Port Authority and the Police Commissioner. No one could have imagined the plan that Sonia had up her sleeve. She had taken care to see that John's drink was heavily laced with opium, which was readily available. Around midnight, when most of the guests were well in their cups heavily drunk and John quite unconscious, she signaled to some servants to take John to the bedroom so he could sleep the drink off. The servants, by previous arrangement, carried him off to a waiting car, which sped to the dock where the ship was moored. Within minutes, Sonia had bidden a hasty farewell to one and all and followed John to the ship. The ship soon weighed anchor and left the port.

No one realized that John was missing

next day. Christina thought that he was probably sleeping off a hangover, this being the first party he had been to in India. She waited till noon. No sign of John. She then went to his room and found that his bed had not been slept in. Dr. Walls was still sleeping, having had too much to drink. He had dreaded meeting Mrs. Desquin after the loss of her husband, and had been utterly charming and polite all evening. He was now completely exhausted and deep in sleep.

Christina did not want to wake up Dr. Walls. She did not know what to do or think. She went back to work, hoping John would return as usual.

Sonia had John laid on a majestic bed in the most magnificent cabin on the ship. John, still drugged, had been married to Sonia by the ship's captain, and Sonia had a passport with the name "Sonia de Montaigne" in her possession at last. She waited for the break of dawn to play her last card, after which she could be sure that her future was secure.

John awoke at noon. Sonia had taken care to see that a hearty breakfast was served in bed to him. When he awoke, he found her in bed beside him, wiping his face with a damp towel. When he demanded where he was, she replied, "Darling, be still. You had a high fever yesterday. Since you fell off the horse, I have been in despair. Your father and mine have both passed away. I have been looking after you."

John, who had forgotten his life at the hospital but did remember that he had worked with her father, asked her, "But when did all this happen?"

Sonia realized that her story was not quite accurate and ventured, "Well, you did work with my father for some months, but you have been indisposed for six months now."

John was sorry that his dear Sonia had had to endure all by herself the death of their two parents, as well as take care of him. He said, "Darling, I am so sorry you had to go through all this without me to help you, but I shall make it up to you."

Sonia added maliciously, "The doctors advised me to take you away to a dry climate. I have sold all of my father's estate, and we are now on our way to America."

John burst out laughing on hearing the word America, saying, "Whatever am I going to do in America?"

Sonia, glad that John had not seen through her stratagem, continued, "My darling, do not worry. I have taken care of everything. We will buy a tea export and import company. We have enough money, thank God."

John, still not completely free of the drug, continued to repeat "America" and laugh in amusement. He ate his breakfast with a voracious appetite and went back to sleep. It took him a few days to be his old self again and for the drug to wear off.

The ship, meanwhile, was slowly sailing west. John hazily remembered the trip that had brought him to India and decided that this trip was altogether much more pleasant. The entire crew treated him like royalty. After all, Sonia had hired the entire ship for herself and John. They were the most precious cargo that this captain had ever carried. John had said to Sonia, "You made a good decision. I hope you never have to regret it. You actually sacrificed your entire estate and your father's fortune to save my life! I will never forget it!" John was impressed by Sonia's gesture of love and her devotion to him, and he was determined to make her as happy as he possibly could. Sonia was in Heaven with the knowledge that her plan had worked. She had John to herself, as she had wanted all along. The trip was long, and John spent his time between the crew members and the captain. He never wondered why they were alone on the vessel, for Sonia never left him by himself for a moment. Every time he wanted to speak about India, she turned the subject to their plans for America.

The trip was one long honeymoon. Sonia had lost no time, and when they disembarked in America she was carrying John's child. John had completely forgotten the past and India; his main concern was to take the best care of his pregnant wife. Sonia enjoyed being treated like a queen.

When Christina saw that a few weeks went by without any sign of John, she was terribly concerned. She thought that maybe John had gone back to Sonia's estate, so she decided to pay them a visit. When she arrived at the estate, she found that a new family had already taken up residence at the mansion and could not help her with her inquiries. Now she was concerned not only for John but for Sonia as well. She tried to elicit some response from Dr. Walls, but he was perpetually drunk and unconcerned about anything except where his next drink was coming from. She visited Mrs. Desquin, who asked her tearfully, "Do you know my husband passed away?" Christina saw that Mrs. Desquin was suffering from a nervous breakdown and returned in frustration to the hospital. She was now determined to work for the sick, who really needed her help.

When John and Sonia arrived in the United States, John was astounded at the care his wife had taken over every detail. She had never disclosed the lengths to which she had gone to make everything perfect for their life in the United States. She had had a close friend of her father buy an estate for them and had bought the giant corporation, American Tea Inc., with which John and her father had traded in the past. Their home was as elegant as a castle, with the best hired help that money could buy, including a butler. John was flabbergasted to see what Sonia could accomplish without any help. He had never suspected that her many talents included business. But he dared not question her. When she hugged him and asked him if he liked their new home, he did not know what to say. During dinner, there was another surprise waiting for him. The table was laid for twenty people. John did not know who these guests were. Soon, Sonia introduced them as the managers of American Tea Inc., the most prestigious company in the world. John listened to her, lost in admiration. He raised his crystal glass and said, "To America!"

After dinner, John was exhausted from the long trip and wanted to sleep. Every one of his managers came up and greeted him, as if he were the chief executive. John felt that he must surely be dreaming. He retired to his bedroom. Sonia, who had sworn never to leave him alone, joined him. They slept through the night like two children.

Within a few weeks, John was already in command of American Tea Inc. With his natural aptitude, his fortune grew considerably. Sonia became the mother of six children, three boys and three girls, and they had a happy family life. John was happy in his new role and never spoke about India. His children grew up healthily, and they were all well loved by their neighbors. Well-placed and affluent people were happy to have them for friends. John travelled frequently, as he had done before. Every year travelling became more comfortable; there were trains, cars, and then planes, which became the new luxury for rich men like John. John became the epitome of a nobleman and enjoyed tremendous respect in business circles.

Sonia felt secure. No one could take John away from her. Years passed. John changed gradually. He became arrogant and very smug with his success. Sonia, in her devious and cunning way, always succeeded in getting what she wanted.

On John's sixtieth birthday, Sonia planned the most elaborate party of her life in the Crystal Ballroom of a luxury hotel, to celebrate the success of her plans. The party went as planned, but Sonia, who loved her social life, decided to continue the party at her mansion with her closest friends. All that evening she never guessed anything about John and the message scribbled on a small piece of paper. Sonia was drunk and laughing hysterically. No one guessed that she was thinking how well her plan had worked, how she had succeeded in marrying John without his knowledge or consent. No one had ever doubted her sincerity. God, how funny!

CONCLUSION

John was still in the ballroom reading the note again and again. These were the words, "Don't build your life on a spider's web." Suddenly all was as clear as daylight to him. He remembered everything. Every detail of his life in India was as apparent to him, as if it had happened only yesterday. He remembered Josephine and Christina, Dr. Walls, and the people sick with cholera, and Dr. Desquin. He did not return home that evening. He ordered all his managers to come to the office. It was a little before four o'clock in the morning. When all were in place, he instructed them to transfer all his fortune to India, in the name of John's Hospital. While no one understood what John was doing, they dared not disobey his orders. Maybe it was a big tea deal, thought his General Manager. He gave a large sum of money to each of his staff, enough to settle them for life. At noon, he sent a message to his wife that he would be travelling for a week on business. This much time was required for him to liquidate his estate. He put up his home as collateral for cash. A week later, he flew to London, then to Cairo, Karachi and Bombay.

The hospital was still the same. Christina was still there, old but very active. She did not recognize him until he began to speak, and then her whole being began to tremble. She looked deep into his eyes and she recognized John. He was old, but this had not changed her feelings and her love for him.

www.ingramcontent.com/pod-product-compliance
Lightning Source LLC
Chambersburg PA
CBHW070600300426
44113CB00010B/1339